THE
BIPOLAR
CODE

A MEMOIR OF UNRAVELING, NAVIGATING, AND EMPOWERING THE BIPOLAR MIND

BY

BOB STAVNITSKI

STAVNITSKI, BOB, Author
THE BIPOLAR CODE
BOB STAVNITSKI
TheBipolarCode.com

Published by
ELITE ONLINE PUBLISHING
63 East 11400 South #230
Sandy, UT 84070
EliteOnlinePublishing.com

ISBN - 978-1-961801-50-9 (Paperback)
ISBN - 978-1-961801-51-6 (eBook)

BIO026000
HEA055000

QUANTITY PURCHASES: Schools, companies, professional groups, clubs, and other organizations may qualify for special terms when ordering quantities of this title. For information, email info@eliteonlinepublishing.com.

"To some extent, sanity is a form of conformity. People are always selling the idea that people who have mental illness are suffering. But it's really not so simple. I think mental illness or madness can be an escape also."

–John F. Nash

The Nobel Laureate portrayed by Russell Crowe in the film "A Beautiful Mind."

For resources and free download
visit TheBipolarCode.com

TABLE OF CONTENTS

DEDICATION

The Bipolar Code is dedicated to the millions of individuals like me who live with bipolar disorder, experience depression and mania, and whose lives long or short have been impacted by a mental illness. I believe for many amongst us that an overall sustainable, happy, creative, even occasionally inspired life experience shared with others is possible through the lens of a bipolar brain. I hope those challenged with mood disorder might derive some insight, hope, and maybe even a little inspiration from my experience.

This is also dedicated to all of our parents, loved ones, friends, and caregivers, all the people whose lives time and again have been interrupted by the calamities resulting from our bipolar disorder. Witnesses to events they find hard to fathom happening right before their eyes in their own homes. Those who find themselves repeatedly heart broken, losing sleep, and lost in a quandary over what to do, and how to help their very sick child, partner, sister, brother, or friend find their way through the self-destructive and complicated web we weave in our bipolar brains.

This story is also dedicated to my own family and predecessors going back to my grandparents, parents, aunts & uncles, siblings, cousins, and especially my wife. As I deconstruct my psychosis with the backdrop of our family tree and our communities, the life and times of key figures along my journey are revealed in the pages of this memoir. Three generations of relatives, close friends, colleagues, even neighbors have witnessed my brushes with madness, none of whom ever made me feel marginalized or as if they had given up on me.

A dedication is also in order for my clinical care team of excellent professionals, psychiatrists, therapists, primary care physicians, pharmacists, and others over the years who have helped me achieve success in my treatment. I would also like to express gratitude to thousands of volunteers in countless organizations who have advocated, educated, and enthusiastically pursued the destigmatization of mental illness from which I have benefited.

Finally, recognizing the ultimate sad reality that bipolar disorder and depression unchecked can be deadly, *The Bipolar Code* is dedicated to those we have lost to suicide. God bless them and their families. Let's all have high hopes that continued improved research, education, access, and curated care can help stem the tide of these gut-wrenching goodbyes.

–Bob Stavnitski

CHAPTER 1

THESE DAYS

As final deadlines from my editor are looming over this effort, I'm getting cold feet. Following a few weeks with the proposed book cover in hand, enlarged on a poster board, I cringed with the realization that an equally appropriate, perhaps more succinct title for "The Bipolar Code" could simply be "ME!" In all caps, even. "ME," I thought, "A self-laudatory memoir of my experience with bipolar disorder." Could I be indulging in a delusion of grandeur? I found myself temporarily stopped in my tracks for the first time, sharing these bipolar ruminations. My confidence in the process suddenly waned. I thought about the reality of penning a memoir as inherently self-promotional and have taken pause to consider this. Notoriety in most forms is considered distasteful to my family. For us, a proper personal public narrative is limited to a birth notice, marriage, athletic achievement, a hole in one, and a discreet obituary. The sum total of our lifetime efforts intended to make a positive impact on others without drawing attention to ourselves.

I'll rationalize that had I ever thought I might gain any lifetime notoriety, calling myself out publicly as mentally ill is not the way I would have planned it. Given the arch of my life, this share is, I believe, the ultimate outcome of what I have been through. Albeit it is an unexpected turn.

Having recently passed my milestone sixtieth birthday, for the past twenty years or more, my team of physicians, therapists, and other caregivers concur, I am essentially healed and in longtime recovery in as much as that is possible for anyone living with bipolar disorder, which never really goes into remission. Professionals share that I have an extremely acute sense for weaving through my own brand of bipolarity. The overall theme of my recent musings that I hope will make a difference is as follows: Whether you live with a mood disorder or someone you love is sick and has become the scary stranger in the house, know that I, and millions of other amazing souls who live with bipolar disorder or manic-depressive disease, as it's also known, we find truth and beauty in the human condition that others with "normal" brains miss out on. Our minds often present with a heightened cognitive sense of empathy for man, art, nature, science, sport, history, philosophy, and spirituality, and the threads that tie these experiences together over the course of a lifetime. Inevitably, it is a complex web we weave in our minds.

I embrace my bipolarity, approaching life through what I know is an emotionally skewed looking glass, like a prism. It is as if I'm wearing prescription glasses that deliver information to my brain in a more complex way than it comes to most people. Bipolarity is a perspective on life through a different lens. The key in the bipolar lens isn't focus as much as it is a tint of the lens, which changes in a metaphoric pattern of colors as our moods cycle. Bipolar disorder is colorful, beautiful, even brilliant. Sometimes, light bulbs go off illuminating the bipolar mind in cool ways. Bipolar individuals are often successful in any endeavor they tackle. Great figures in history were bipolar, as are some of your neighbors.

The healthy rose-colored lens of the bipolar mind is a slightly more creative and happier perspective on life than most other people enjoy. Unfortunately, it's a place that can be elusive and difficult to maintain. When our moods swing to depression, our rose-colored glasses veer from a happy pale pink to somber blue. A long, seemingly unending depression is oh so bad.

The third shade, however, is worse. In shorter bursts and far more dramatic and expensive are the manic episodes. It's as if the tint of glasses through which the bipolar brain experiences the day fades from the morose shade of blue or happy or relaxed pink, *to psychedelic*. Mania is like experiencing life through the lens of a kaleidoscope. Everything is colorful, bright, constantly changing, and fast. The enthusiasm, creativity, and the in-overdrive emotion feel like an imaginary light switch has been turned on. Suddenly, we see all things crystal clear. We can change the world. Mania is fun, exciting, and empowering. It's also overwhelming, difficult to stop, and dangerous. To our own detriment, most bipolar individuals love the manic phases.

Imagine that the soundtrack of the manic mind is "The Flight of the Bumblebee." It's loud and fast, increasing with speed and on all the time. If you can corner your bipolar loved one or friend in that manic phase long enough to inquire what's going on, you might find yourself thinking, If only we could bottle that emotion and channel every great bipolar notion into a solution, maybe we would have a cure for cancer or the common cold, born out of the madness.

Yes, there is beauty in the bipolar mind, but it's probably better characterized as beauty and an emotionally brutal beast. A beast that can turn deadly left unchecked. If you are bipolar and going through it, or if you love someone who is suffering, there is hope. The brutal beast can be tamed. A happy, successful, hopes and dreams do come true kind of life, as a member of a family and a contributing member of a community is possible. That's what happened to me.

In the early pages of this memoir, I divert from my downhill slide, sharing, admittedly at length, detailed biographies of the core individuals of my family. Bear with me; all of this background is important as it represents the recipe for my bipolarity. It's not groundbreaking to suggest that family history from all sides are the spiritual, intellectual, environmental, emotional, and socioeconomic building blocks for all of us. In the case of those with broken minds, these connections can be triggers for psychosis, whereas a thorough understanding of these relationships can lead to wisdom and recovery. I am pleased, at least for a while as you read, that this story is not just absolutely all about me. I hope some of you will recognize yourselves or your own loved ones in the likes of our family.

At the outset, I want to be clear that this memoir describes my perspective on becoming bipolar, which is a continuing evolution, and l how I live with it, nothing more. I am sharing experience, not counsel, and certainly not medical advice. This comes from the heart rather than through the benefit of textbooks. Both my education and my business life have been considerably curtailed as a result of mood disorder.

To put my educational career into perspective, I am currently on a 45-year-plus program for a bachelor's degree. I have completed, or better put, attended 264 credit hours' worth of higher education at several well-known institutions, mainly in old-school liberal arts programs. I have definitely spent more than enough time in the classroom to have earned multiple degrees, maybe even a PhD. Unfortunately, I've never been able to put everything in the right order to apply for graduation. Since dropping out of college for the first time in my early twenties, it has been like climbing the Himalayas to finish a degree at a bricks-and-mortar institution.

I am confident my serpentine weave through four universities has provided me with more education than many folks I've come across with lots of abbreviations behind their names. This is not a brag, not something of which I am proud. In fact, I'm a little bit embarrassed by it. Considering this, I wonder what the grand total cost of all the money I spent on tuition, room, and board would amount to. Beyond that, I wonder what the long-term opportunity and lifestyle cost has been in terms of lost income and quality of life, even perhaps increased intellectual pursuits I might have enjoyed had I completed at least a minimum of a bachelor's degree. Perhaps it is impossible to put a close enough estimate on it, and not sure that would be a productive exercise. Still, I do not regret any of it. Education of any kind is never a waste. After all of the starts and stops, I suppose the correct way to refer to my level of academic achievement is self-educated and ongoing.

Although, to be honest, as I pen this, my lack of credentials as well as my oft wandering mind make me worry that the writing of this long train of thought might lack sensibility. Without a doubt, my literary style here represents page after page of an absolute masterpiece of grammatical incorrectness. I am not oblivious to the fact that my conversational format contains one run-on sentence after another, and I worry readers may take a bit to get used to this. Frequently, my run-on ramblings are capped off with dubious incomplete sentences. I cannot imagine the number of red pens my former teachers and professors would go through should they ever grade this. It reminds me of our junior high English classes when we were taught how to diagram a sentence, which was just as bad as algebra as far as I was concerned.

I enjoy my propensity for alliteration in both writing and conversation, but not sure my use of it is an indulgence of a literary tool that is as palatable for today's readers. The way I write for you here, in my affected brain feels "pronounc'd trippingly on the tongue," as Shakespeare would have it, at least to me. I am keen to provide a true glimpse into how mood disorder feels, and my rambling prose here itself is possibly the ultimate expression of a bipolar brain at work.

Separate from bipolarity, I have always maintained an intensely precise chronological autobiographic memory. Everyone who knows me well enough will concur that I have an extraordinary memory for everything from milestones to minutia. No doubt as I've aged, memories are enhanced, intertwined, with some key details and ideas having been both omitted or elaborated upon. I may not get everything one hundred percent anymore, but I'm confident I get the gist of most old memories pretty much spot on, at least close enough for me. I expect some family members reflections of some of the stories I share here are divergent from mine. Either way, I'm convinced that putting in context all of these threads from my life and accompanying threads from the lives of my predecessors and others provides a roadmap to some wisdom and some understanding of who we are and what our tiny place in the universe is all about. Understanding these ties that bind the fabric of our lives, whether with family or friends, has been a great motivator in my recovery. I also personally feel this kind of total recall is a cool way to experience life and the people I share it with.

Given the consistency of my memory, I have tried to use restraint in the recounting of too much family folklore and antidotes in hopes of avoiding any impression of reading on about us, "to last syllable of recorded time." I know there are those who consider my memory of the past to be boring. I am also aware that this kind of memory has a bearing on my ability to live in the moment, as well as focus on the future, a knack I am trying to kick. Still, as you read, I beg you to consider one man's mundanity as another man's sport. Finding joy in others and sometimes wonder in life's mundane moments are in large part the key to recovery and, ultimately, happiness.

Not long ago, I had been asked to develop a TEDx presentation. "Hello, my name is Bob, and I am bipolar." was my opening Gambit. "Yes, I am bipolar, but that's not all." My father's family has a strong history of mental illness going back at least three generations, and we would be naive not to assume further beyond that in our ancestry. Eventually, mood disorder has wielded a profound impact on our most recent group of cousins and extended family.

Although I'm obviously partial, all of this has happened, sadly and cross-generationally, to a family of kind, charming, thoughtful, wise, funny, involved people. They are eager, enthusiastic, faithful, educated, family and civic-minded, highly social, and entrepreneurial, all with a strong work ethic, and include many special individuals whose lives have been interrupted, as has mine, by mental illness.

We have managed to cast a wide net of people in both our social and professional spheres, most of whom I'm sure would be shocked to hear that amongst us, even recently, we have experienced deep depression, manic episodes, major anxiety, drug abuse, overdoses, avoidable accidents, suicides, DUI's, arrests, hospitalizations, involuntary committals and otherwise, incarcerations, rehabs, restraining orders, dysfunctional holidays and birthdays (these were often my specialty), and more than one major family event we remember especially due to the psychotic breakdowns that happened before our eyes as we gathered to celebrate or mourn. As the old saying goes, we have swept this under the rug. I'm not sure if this is motivated more by good manners rather than saving face.

We are committed husbands and wives, mothers and fathers, grandparents, brothers and sisters, cousins, can be wonderful friends to others, and even with all of the emotional baggage that mental illness can bring to bear upon a family, we love hard on each other, it's the only way we know. Some lay in wait, having said goodbye to their best lives yet remain hopeful for happier times ahead. Others have beaten their demons in wonderful ways. Some seem to surrender, perhaps too sick to prosper. When our hearts are broken, we discovered it's best to avoid, in our case, our old Catholic habits of casting aspersion and judgment. No use in making each other feel guilty or ashamed, we've found this completely unproductive. Bipolarity is no one's fault or choice. Those who go through it wish it upon no one.

My mother's family, on the other hand, had no history of mental illness, not one scintilla. Indeed, their history is a storybook rendition of achievement, success, and sometimes position. They could hardly believe their eyes witnessing the behavior and resulting carnage in the lives of their loved ones. They were completely shocked by these crippling life interruptions and were ill-equipped to understand or manage. So, my TEDx talk morphed instead into a memoir, a tribute that lovingly describes both my father's and my mother's families. It also describes the perfect storm of mental illness that ensued when my parents married.

These days, I experience life through rose-colored glasses. I believe others with brains like mine can do it, too. Keeping the bipolar beast at bay does not happen by accident. It takes the love of self and others, faith, hope, ownership, fortitude, courage, education, medication, nutrition, dedication, and so much more to achieve bipolar emancipation. It's also an inbred promise that all this effort to maintain a level personal approach will still suck the life out of us from time to time. So, add perseverance to the list of key traits for success. Sometimes, we all just need to dust ourselves off when we fall and get back up on the horse. Sadly, recovery won't happen for every family. Still, with continued discoveries about the workings of the human brain, the world of modern medicine, and the continuing destigmatization of mental illness, the odds for all of us are better and improving.

CHAPTER 2

MY BIPOLAR ONSET

In the 80's, they referred to my bipolar onset for a guy starting at age 18-20 as textbook. In high school, like my father, I sailed through life like everybody's All-American. My parents were over-the-moon proud and expected the very best for my future; everyone we knew did.

Then, for many years after that, it all crashed. My childhood string of successes ended abruptly for a very long time, until my eventual diagnosis at age thirty-three, even for many years beyond that. By that time, I had become a two-time college dropout and had unknowingly suffered depression through four sales positions. I was fired from two of them. I felt like I had peaked in high school.

As a bona fide mentally ill guy, I've been fortunate in my life. I've managed to carve out an interesting career path, if not a lucrative one. No doubt, my career has fallen short of the level of success that was anticipated for me as a young man, not only by my parents but by teachers, coaches, and friends. Even at my reduced level of accomplishment, with persistence, I still managed to win many local, regional, and national sales awards with plaques and trips to show for it. I eventually had the opportunity to travel the world on business. But I never managed to hit the expected mark. I never achieved the kind of reach that we thought exhibited my full potential.

In addition to my academic failures, it's cringeworthy to admit that I can count nineteen jobs in my career. Over the years, I have been fired nine times in total. Each time was like a death. I've been hired, fired, and re-hired twice by two different excellent companies. I've kept a string of friends from all my old jobs and more than once left behind a good boss saddened to have had to let me go. I was highly effective and profitable, and I usually managed to make the workplace fun until the maniacal workload I created would spin out of control.

My madness was most prominently expressed in professional situations. In my early working years, it took every ounce of effort to get up on time every Monday through Friday, put on a tie, and work 9-5 under the pressure of deadlines and sales quotas. Otherwise, I existed quietly. I would go home, comfort, eat, and, for the most part, go directly to bed on weeknights. Over the weekend, I would not get out of bed at all. Although I typically had a decent apartment in a good community, some pretty bad bachelor housekeeping eventually verged on hoarding. Lots of pizza boxes, piles of mail, strewn around food and clothing, newspapers, gross kitchens, and bathrooms. I managed a bit of a social life, but my primary companions were on prime-time television and re-runs. I rarely let anyone into any of my homes.

A personal sustaining grace for me during my twenties and thirties and beyond was always and has always been my relationship with my parents. I've been fortunate to maintain enduring ties with my family throughout my entire bipolar experience. I know this is not the case for everyone. My mother and father were a great couple. Both were successful, motivated, and well-respected. Regardless of my surprising, recurring difficulties and setbacks, they continued to expect accomplishment. They never gave up on me, and this was a great enablement. I have never given up on myself, in large part because of their persistent confidence in me.

Although they rarely demonstrated it, all three of us knew that my life and the way things were going for me as a young guy, had become their own biggest lifetime disappointment. I was definitely underachieving. Until things went sour for me, nothing had really ever gone wrong for my parents. I was the baby son, the one of their three kids upon whom they had laid all their hopes and expectations for the future, but I was falling seriously, repeatedly, short. They lost sleep over me night after night, year after year.

Until I hit my late teens, I had the "it" factor big time. But by my thirties, fifteen years of disappointment were approaching. Despite all the clues, we were completely oblivious. I sat through frequent teary-eyed parental lectures, just the three of us at our family dinner table. Oddly, it never occurred to any of us that I was suffering from mental illness.

We did not think that happened in "good" families like ours. It was not in our frame of reference, even given the fact that my paternal grandmother, a wonderful person, was lovingly known by all of us as different. A great lady, but definitely "off." I learned later from aunts, uncles, and cousins that our grandma, who was widely beloved and admired despite her disease, slept through a lot of the '60s and '70s, sedated by Valium and Quaalude's prescribed by psychiatrists to manage her moods. When depressed, she was taking the uppers we used to call speed. In those days, we were not as close to my dad's side of our family. We were hundreds of miles away, years separated. No one connected grandma's strange behavior to my issues. I am not projecting blame for anyone's mental illness upon grandma. In fact, perhaps more than I have, she beat her demons through fortitude and made a difference in a multitude of people's lives.

It's very difficult for loved ones, friends, and caregivers who witness a lot of the crazed behavior firsthand; it's hard to place themselves in the footsteps of someone going through a bipolar mental health crisis.

My folks certainly couldn't do it. So, I'm going to take a few deep breaths, in through the nose, out through the mouth, as we are taught in therapy, and explain out loud the events surrounding my one major breakdown and what it was like to go through it.

You should understand that my entire family, my mother, father, and my beloved late Grandparents would aggressively and in unison object to this public airing of private family business. "Absolutely not!" "How dare you!" are doubtless anticipated responses. Rightfully so. Even close friends or virtual ones would suggest that talking about your family secrets, mental illness, and money is vulgar. What's even worse is writing about one's own money, especially if you've got a lot of it. These things are held close. And yet, my family's wealth, what folks refer to as old money, is in large part the backdrop of my story.

As difficult as my beautiful bipolar journey has been, I can't imagine what it would have been like to go through it without the benefit of solid, go-to financial resources and higher education. My family, as well as most of our friends, enjoyed both of those benefits. Higher education provides better odds for understanding and coming to grips with mental illness and provides the intellectual tools to weave through the healthcare system and get good help. I'm confident that anyone who manages to come out on the other side under more meager circumstances than I have been granted is far stronger than I am. I should credit my grandmother for this accomplishment.

Pondering what I am certain would be my family's reaction, I wonder how frank I'm really going to be here. How much of my own personal business do I want to share before I violate my own privacy? As this evolves from a motivational talk for bipolar patients and caregivers to my personal tome, am I really willing to incriminate myself in this way? Mental illness does not discriminate or bring out the best in us. Rather, it affects us at our cores like cancer. Bipolar disorder is not for sissies.

When I went through the worst of it in the 80s and 90s, many friends and relatives still did not get it or even believe in it. No surprise. There was a greater stigma then; less knowledge was available. On a superficial level, I was generally able to successfully keep up appearances. But in close relationships, most did not understand me. I lost a lot of friends permanently in those years. It took even more years afterward to realize that losing friendships is typical, with even a little bit of madness. It's inevitable, and it's OK. I've learned most friendships are built upon geography anyway.

By the age of 35, although clearly short of my full potential, I had reached a modicum of personal and professional success. I was catching up. I was a few years removed from my first firing from a successful award-winning run in the Yellow Page business selling advertising, which came to a disappointing conclusion. I rebounded and was a couple years into a pretty good position with a local commercial and residential security company selling security equipment to school districts, manufacturers, and prominent businesses in our hometown. I'd won trips to Nashville and San Antonio. I'd even recently won another national sales award, the first ever for our hometown franchise. I had a happy boss. I was making him lots of money. I was earning the best money in my life, certainly enough to keep up appearances, and I was behind the wheel of a nice new Honda Accord. In a first out-of-character clue, in a choice my parents had warned against, I purchased an investment property, a four-unit, 75-year-old apartment building with tenants in the nice neighborhood close to the house in which I had grown up and right down the street from our high school. I moved into one of the units and was landlord to two friends from school.

I also followed a fifty-year family tradition and became a member of our local country club. I became a fourth-generation member of the local Rotary Club. Finally, because bosses in the 1990's really encouraged community involvement, I became a Chamber of Commerce event committee chair. At this point, it seemed like things were really starting to come together for me. My parents' only regular complaint was my lack of a relationship with a nice girl or marriage. We were constantly going to fancy weddings. My mother went on and on about marriage and their desire for grandchildren: "Who are you dating? Are you ever going to get married? Give us grandchildren?" And, since by this time, I was about ten years into my battle with food, the marriage refrain was shortly joined with the question, "When are you going to lose weight?" and "Don't eat that,"

At this point, a disclaimer on my parents' behalf is in order. While for decades, our conversations were laced with Catholic guilt, raised voices, and disappointment, I never questioned their love, devotion, and overall goodwill and hopeful hearts for me in life. Even when things were tough between us, I liked them. I was proud of them. I was proud to be their son. I was one of the lucky ones. They just did not know what to do when I became a stranger to them. My bipolar disorder strained our relationship, but we never became estranged.

During the summer of '96, to put this in perspective, it was the summer of the Atlanta Olympics bombing, and I was slowly descending into the deepest depression of my life. I did not understand it as depression, but I was familiar with the emotion. For the first time, it was not going away. Weekend after weekend, I would only leave the house to head out for fast food, bringing home huge sacks of junk food. I would then eat it all in one, sitting in bed in front of a black-and-white television. I couldn't bring myself to go to the golf course which I had just joined. I never really liked golf, but the pool there, which I loved and had been captain of the swim team in my glory days, was still crowded with friends. Normally, I would be all about that pool, but I had no interest in it. Easily 40 pounds overweight (or more), I was embarrassed to be seen in public with my shirt off.

I was also losing my eloquence, which had always been somewhat noteworthy. Any success I managed was no doubt tied to a decent amount of personal charm and presence, a deep, clear voice, and a great sense of humor. All these things were eluding me. Finally, my mood evolved into darkness, loneliness, and stark sadness.

I suppose you asked friends and family, though, everything that summer seemed to be going well because like the rest of my family, I had a knack for putting my best foot forward. We performed well in public regardless of our feelings. My folks taught us this by example. However, by September, I could no longer cover it, especially on the job. The smallest of professional decisions, ones I could usually make with ease, became insurmountable mountains. My personal appearance, in addition to my size, clothing, and shoes, appeared ill-kempt. That nice Honda was heaped with paperwork, empty food wrappers, and an ashtray overflowing with cigarette butts. My apartment was a dirty wreck, smelling like old food, dirty laundry, and smoke. My nice tenants were not getting basic things fixed in an old building. I had also recently taken on an adult beagle rescue. "Chipper" loved me dearly, and I him, but I was in no position to care for myself, let alone a pet. My apartment began to reek of dog pee. Even today, merely describing these events causes the same old emotions to appear again.

The one gratifying effort of that era of darkness and depression was the creation of a garden at my semi-dilapidated apartment complex. Because it was located on a relatively busy corner, with cheery municipal "our town" kinds of banners and planters of geraniums hung on light posts, the yard needed attention. After all, children walked to school, moms pushed strollers, and joggers frequented the sidewalks in a steady, preppy stream.

When I bought the place, the yard and grounds were old scruffy hedges, with overgrown brush, vines, and weeds everywhere. I planted a perennial garden and border for the public view, cut back some trees, and pulled ivy from the brick. Aside from persistent dandelions, I took decent care of the lawn. Hours of yard work was my only physical exertion.

Soon, the yard and garden became a sunny display of pale-yellow moonbeam coreopsis, purple sage, salvia, purple iris, and golden sedum. Under the brush, I found heirloom peonies, various hosta, and lilies of the valley. I even planted a spring display of crocus, colorful hyacinth, daffodils, and bright red and yellow tulips. The beautiful part of my bipolar brain was expressed in bloom. I spent many hours tending plants, watering, and chatting with lots of old family friends who passed by as I did the yard work. I had started jokingly referring to the place as "the slum." My father often said, "There is truth in all humor," and he was right because the building was beaten up relative to the neighborhood.

With the garden, I was able to maintain the outward appearance as a pulled together good neighbor, and the neighborhood appreciated it. The inside of the dilapidating structure, however, was definitely more attuned with my state of mind as my depression deepened.

As these memories unfold, I should add a reinforcing disclaimer that might cast aspersion on my recovery as, in any way, laudatory. Simply put, that disclaimer is affluence. Although this is not what I was going through myself, the term affluenza was trending at the time. Affluenza: a psychological malaise affecting wealthy youth, symptoms of which include a lack of motivation and a sense of isolation. In other words, I felt a plain and simple rationalization for someone whose life was not living up to their entitled expectations. My first depression felt this way, but my problems were deeper.

Relative to our community's concentration of wealth, even in that frame of reference, our family was well off. Yet my parents were tremendously discreet, and no one suspected that my family had money. As children, we did not suspect it ourselves, even throughout our teens. My parents lived on tight budgets and made zero pretentions.

Growing up, our family home was not on the estate side of town, but in a section of town that realtors later called the Golden Triangle. We loved our home and yard and were proud of it. I was ten when we moved into it in 1973, and it was a big upgrade beyond what we ever thought a house would be like for us. A two-and-a-half-story white pillared 1920s sort of Greek revival transitioning to craftsman set up with double French doors opening onto a wide covered front porch, a great third-floor finished attic room with great views for my brother and me. There was a small, detached carriage house turned garage. A great spooky basement with an old coal chute, all on an oversized lot with a giant pine and a massive blooming catalpa tree, both providing a great climb, shade, and privacy.

The house was a good size, not too big, tastefully appointed with a lot of what people used to call parents' provincial furnishings, great hand-me-downs from grandma & grandpa. It was updated within reason, perfectly maintained, and hospital clean. My parents drove a carpooling station wagon or Buick Le Sabre and Oldsmobile Delta Eighty-Eights while our dad's business partners drove long Cadillac Sedan De Villes. Dad did get a new company car every other year. All three of us kids knew we had more than most outside our neighborhood, but our parents frequently made it crystal clear this was not our achievement nor any of our business. They preached that advantage came with extremely high expectations and responsibility.

My parents had their own goals, dreams, and visions for their lives. Their existence did not revolve exclusively around their children. They were delightful together and drew tremendous numbers of people into their lives and ours. They were a very social couple, well-liked and well-respected, with no blips on the radar screen, and they had the outward appearance of a model family. That's how it felt to me at the time. They loved traveling for business and pleasure. Both enjoyed their own individual groups at the golf club and had a busy social life together.

These were separate from us kids. They pursued them enthusiastically and put a tremendous amount of time and effort into their own goings-on as a couple. Through it all, neither of them ever missed a school event, concert, game, or play. Their support was indefatigable. They hauled us to Mass on Sunday. Every week, mother prepared a proper Sunday family dinner in the formal dining room, which was normally served on China, always using the good silver. In some ways typical, elevated in others.

Mom and Dad conducted a daily weekday happy hour wrap-up in the kitchen, Mother over the stove with a scotch and soda, Dad just home from the office drinking a Miller Light and snacking on Del Monte Chili Peppers. Through most of the 70s, both of them puffed pretty heavily on Tareyton cigarettes. Once they had had their moment, we kids would be called to sit at our stools at the Formica bar peninsula for a really good, wholesome home cooked dinner. The five of us together almost every weeknight.

All three of us progeny were expected to produce academically, participate in extracurricular activities (and be winners), earn our own money, be kind and truthful, and never do anything wrong. My sister was a great babysitter and later a waitress, and an accomplished floutist, her daily rehearsals were our home's soundtrack. Lawn mowing, paper routes, and caddying fell to my brother and me; those things we did begrudgingly but faithfully. Mom collected and doled out our profits sparingly, stashing the remainder in manilla envelopes stored on a secret shelf in her closet. Each entry, credit and debit, perfectly logged for our future college spending money.

Mom was a prominent volunteer civic leader as a stay-at-home, traditional wife, homemaker, hostess, and semi-retired registered nurse. She was tall, just on the edge of buxom as a young mother, dieting and walking to stay successfully thin, notably pretty. She had a beautiful smile and hazel blue eyes that radiated with what my old girlfriends would later call her signature red lipstick. She was very well educated, eloquent, elegant, sweet, laid back, and could be formal or casual. She enjoyed playing bridge, symphony, ballet, and the opera, and dragged all of us to all of them over the years. Her style was simple and classic. She wore the best of fabrics, perfectly pressed, sensible shoes, minimal makeup, and a proper regular hairdo or permanent. Always, quality over quantity. She preferred to appear tasteful and properly turned out and rarely dressed with the intention of drawing attention to herself. Her black hair was kept stylishly short and faded gradually until her 70s, when she evolved into a stunningly lovely silver fox. Her locks and looks were often commented upon and complimented by strangers. If she had any other signature look, it was good heirloom quality gold and pearls.

In my senior year in high school, my siblings and I realized that my mother was blessed with one other feature that would impact all our lives: she was an heiress to half the estate of a successful self-made industrialist, our grandpa. At that time, the only grandfather we really knew. This was Christmas of 1981, during my undefeated wrestling season, just a few months after he had died from a stroke at age 75. Dressed in blazers, ties, and dresses, waiting for our very traditional, very formal Christmas dinner while the adults held their annual before-Christmas dinner family business cocktail meeting in the kitchen. Figuring it my oldest cousin, siblings, and I turned to each other jaws dropped with the bombshell that grandpa died a very rich man indeed.

There's another reason for figuratively digging up grandpa: I was the one who was supposed to follow in his footsteps. He was a great entrepreneur and businessman. He was a genius, having received a master's degree in chemical engineering from the Massachusetts Institute of Technology. He was very tall, 6 feet 4 inches, very lean, dashingly handsome, and very imposing. He also had a light behind his eyes, a great smile, and a great sense of humor. In most ways, the most successful and charming of all of us, probably by far. Always impeccably and expensively dressed like an old-school dapper gentleman. The scope of his professional and social circles eclipsed that of my parents. His sons-in-law referred to him as Big Robert and his sphere was international, a rarity in his era.

Grandpa's oyster was the world, and I was the one expected to reach for the pearl inside it. I was singled out as "The One" of his grandchildren who was most likely to succeed, and grandpa set the bar very, very high. Therein lies the laying on my shoulders of Mom and Dad's hopes and dreams. Through high school, it seemed all systems were a go. How sad for the whole family and me when in 1985, just two-plus years after grandpa died, I suddenly dropped out, failing badly from the college that both grandpa and his father had graduated from with major honors in 1899 and 1927, respectively.

Not long before I came into the picture, by 1960, grandpa was years into a partnership in a corporation that fostered the "O" Ring industry. Grandma's household, discreet in size yet very tasteful and very elegant, now included a full-time maid and a houseman, who also functioned as the gardener and occasionally their chauffeur. Over the next ten years, Big Robert ingeniously grew his business, building numerous plants eventually employing thousands of people in Ohio, Canada, Tennessee, and even an aerospace division in Phoenix. He patented, manufactured, and sold more than three trillion "O" rings and sparked the industry that continues. He sold the business in 1970, still in its early days, and retired young for his generation, happy to play lots of golf, travel, and entertain with his extremely lovely wife. His inventions and processes are still valid to this day.

CHAPTER 3

MY HERO

I am fortunate to have my Dad's voluminous college scrapbook chronicling his football career. These were his years as "Everybody's All American," the period in his life that continues to define him to this day. Housekeeping disclaimers here. First, when talking to my parents in person, they were always only Mom and Dad. Still, my folks were one of those inseparable, indelible couples simply referred to by all known to us as George & Betsy, so over time, I began to refer to them in public as George and Betsy myself. I will continue to do so here. As I write this, Betsy has been gone for nearly eight years, and George is a good 40% through his journey into the "long goodbye" that is dementia, accompanied by a domino effect of other ailments. These include a treatable but fragile condition called Myelodysplastic Syndrome.

For at least five years now, George has had the benefit of injections of Procrit, which promotes red blood cell production. Recently, our team of oncology nurses has begun to gently suggest that this may not be a humane, long-term solution, given his dementia and major frailty at 86. They fear that his body may be artificially kept going beyond his brain's capacity to manage it.

He resides at a first-class nursing care facility nearby. Luckily, at this point he still knows me as his last link to his former life. As is common, however, his short-term memory is the primary loss. He can still reel a tale from childhood like nobody's business. Although terribly lonely, and often depressed as a result, he remains cheerful and motivated the best he can. Witnessing this, I've never been prouder of him, and never in my life more inspired by him.

George calls me several times a day. All of our often-long conversations eventually come back around to: "Where's my car?" He has not driven in more than four years. "I need some money…Who is going to pay for the hotel bill here?" And "Can I go to the dining room?" Sometimes, he will skip a meal in the nursing home dining room fearing that the certified nursing assistants who serve him will present him with a bill. He calls them waitresses. I carefully manage his financial affairs with the help of a bookkeeper. The concierge at the nursing home occasionally hands me letters he tries to send with cash, responding to ads in the Sunday paper "Parade Magazine" or for insurance co-pay requests that accidentally find their way to him. In return envelopes, regardless of the requested amount, he slips two twenties. I've had to refrain from sharing more than $100 cash with him at a time and have asked the receptionist to only give Dad his sadly very limited personal correspondence and save the rest for me. This makes him feel emasculated, as does the frequent loss of his wallet with identification, driver's license, Medicare card, credit cards, etc. Although he no longer has any need for these items, I know how he feels; I check to ensure my wallet is on me at least twenty times a day. Not having it would freak me out, too.

Our phone calls generally end the same way: "Where do you live? Where am I? Where do I live? When am I going home? Where is my home?" Once he has been redirected on these top-of-mind issues, he gets tearful and reminds me how much he misses his wife Betsy, how wonderful she was, how much she helped him, and how lonely he is without her. Then he finishes off with the sweetest, most grateful, most kind phone call "so longs" a guy could ever hope to get from his father. Sometimes it's hard for me not to cut off his "I love you's" when I hang up.

George was born in what they used to refer to as the "Hunk Town" neighborhood of Bridgeport, Connecticut in 1934, the first son and grandson of enterprising Eastern European immigrants. The ancestral background of this family is shrouded in mystery, much beyond a generation. It seems they fled Europe in bits and pieces around 1900. The only name we've got, that we know of on Ellis Island roles, is George's grandmother, who arrived as Barra Gabor in 1912, having sailed through Southampton, UK. Her country of origin was listed as Austria-Hungary, which, of course, at the time, represented a lot of sovereign nations.

As far as we know, Barra arrived in America by herself with $12.00 US. She spoke Slovenian, so there was that, but never any clues to any place or ancestry. She married a tree surgeon named Dominko, who died young, and soon she became a devout matron of the local Catholic Parish. Turns out this woman was a powerhouse of a lady who gave George's family a secure start in Connecticut. I only met her once for about 15 minutes in 1974. She was lying in bed at a nursing home in Bridgeport. This was during the only vacation trip in the family wagon we ever made to visit George's side of the family. I was 11 years old. I was surprised she spoke in a foreign language during most of our short visit, it would never occur to us that someone in our family would not have English as a first language.

That same afternoon, we trekked to a bar owned by Grandma Dominko's daughter, George's aunt, and our Great-Aunt Bessie. As we pulled to the curb, Betsy turned to the three of us in the back of the packed to the gills family wagon, looked at us in the eyes, and said, "By the way, your Aunt Bessie dresses like a man. Don't say anything about it." And that was that.

None of us kids had ever been to a bar before; this was very exciting. We also met Aunt Bessie's life companion and business partner, Gladys DuBois, a woman Dad told me years later everybody called "Frenchy." The bar had one of those vintage long wooden bumper bowling alley games. Aunt Bessie gave each of us kids a twenty-dollar bill, which none of us had ever even held before. From that, Betsy gave us $3.00 each to spend during the trip; the rest was stowed away for a rainy day. This fleeting, one-time-only visit with George's relatives was the only chance we had to know at least some of these people about whom George reminisced so lovingly and often at the head of our family dining room table in Ohio.

At the time, George's parents owned "Stav's Delicatessen" on the famous Post Road in Fairfield. A modest convenience store with a small deli counter, Grandpa Stav awoke every day in the wee hours to go to the deli and slice traditional hard rolls to be ready for the busy morning rush. The store was full of junk food, soda, and candy. Betsy disapproved of most of this, especially when, on rare occasions, a box of it would arrive for us kids in the mail.

One morning on this trip, George's father, who we called Grandpa Stav, woke us kids up early, and we enjoyed a visit to Stav's Deli with Mr. Stav himself. We were intrigued as he drank a glass of boiling water while he worked. I've never met anyone else ever who drank plain boiling water to start the day. He lived a good, long life, so maybe I should take up his habit. I remember our Grandpa Stav and his sister, Aunt Peg, reminiscing about their days as orphans and sneaking out behind haystacks to smoke cigarettes at very young ages. My brother, sister, and I had never heard of such living. This was definitely eye-opening for us.

Also on the agenda for this trip was a cookout at the home of Aunt Carmel, the Australian war bride George's Uncle Joe Dominko had brought home but later divorced. I'm not sure we met Aunt Carm &

Uncle Joe's son George's younger cousin Stephen "Stevie" Dominko on this junket, but his bio is worth sharing here because his career is definitely one for the record books, and truly reflects the culture of this side of our family.

When accordion popularity was at its height, starting at age 10, he performed groundbreaking concerts in Europe, Australia, even at Carnegie Hall, and his performances were frequently broadcasted, live on television and radio both nationally and globally. Stevie won the US championship at 13, and finally earned the title as the youngest ever world champion accordion player at age 18 in 1965. He was hailed as a genius and prodigy by the great maestro Leonard Bernstein after a live televised virtuoso performance of Chopin's Concerto No 2, 3rd movement, accompanied by the New York Philharmonic at the original Avery Fisher Hall. A YouTube video bears witness to Bernstein's praise of our musically savant cousin Stevie Dominko to a worldwide television audience of millions of viewers on of Bernstein's popular youth concert series. Two albums of classic accordion music are forever by our cousin out there in the world wide web.

Sadly, Stevie lost his sister, his son, and niece, all three to depression. His sister, my father's first cousin, committed suicide Kevorkian style in a hotel room. I was told she suffered from tinnitus and couldn't take the noise anymore. Sadly, it seems, suicides are not uncommon with this condition. Steven's son died young from a gun cleaning accident. His niece, my second cousin, who I was told was paranoid schizophrenic and died young from an overdose, but later learned her suicide was beyond tragic in the way she committed it. I never really got to know these people, but I loved them as family. I once danced at a wedding with my lovely cousin who we lost to tinnitus. It was the only time I ever met her. I will concede the gun cleaning accident as just that, an accident, although more than once, I've seen a grieving especially Catholic mother relieved of guilt by kind law enforcement who deemed their son's suicide accidental.

With all this history in my father's family, the fact that there are some in our extended clan who still deny any genetic predisposition to mental illness is interesting, although perhaps not surprising. Denial is still a predictable cultural response to madness. "It's not in my family," many justify, I think, due to fear of the stigma. At the same time, I cannot judge their response to believe that all is well. It is the same way others respond to any number of illnesses that one cannot judge. All of us react on a gut level to these things, and there should be zero recrimination for other's responses that are contrary to ours.

When and if we disagree, let it be an opportunity to learn from and understand each other, and remember to love each other where we are, not for what we expect from each other. As far as I'm concerned, some dose of bipolar has rubbed off on all of us even for those who are only witnesses to it. And why not celebrate who you are. So, if Stevie were still alive, I'd ask him to break out his accordion and play "Roll out the Barrel!" Given all the life difficulties that have been presented with this side of our family, they soldier on, happily in their niche. They are great fun, kind, loving, smart, and sweet, all of them, and as ever kind and wonderful to me.

George's maternal Dominko side was definitely Slovene, but the paternal Stavnitski ancestral origin remained a mystery until it appeared through the magic of social media. In the 1990s, George started corresponding with a distant cousin, Dorothea, a widowed Connecticut government secretary who loved genealogy and typing. Over the years, she sent George and Betsy perfectly typed, fun, colorful letters and charts but no real clue as to the hometown or our country of origin. Eventually, however, Dorothea's research revealed the name of a village and a photo of it labeled Toporec, Austria-Hungary.

Unfortunately, this caused continued confusion for another twenty or more years. Where is Toporec the old Austro-Hungarian Empire? George, who sees life as very simple, very black and white, had taken to referring to himself when asked as Hungarian, "I'm a Hungarian Prince," he would joke.

It was a search I made not long ago on YouTube that solved the mystery, and in the end, it's quite comical. The search for Toporec, to my amazement, resulted in hundreds of videos taken there. One after the other, all of them are the same thing, showing raucous Gypsy "Svadba's" resembling what might be known here on American TV as "My Big Fat Gypsy Wedding."

The small village of approximately 1800 inhabitants is situated in the foothills of the High Tatra Mountain Range in the Presov district of Northern Slovakia, maybe four hours west of Bratislava by car and two hours south over the mountains from Krakow, Poland. It seems to be a Gypsy wedding destination.

And why not? It is an absolutely beautifully picturesque, aged rural mountain village in a lush green valley with red tile roofs and small discrete onion domes denoting the churches. There are towering snowcapped mountains just a few miles in the distance. It's stunning. The reveal of it after all the years of wondering took my breath away. The beauty of it belies the reality. Whereas, at least from a distance, it looks bucolic and romantic, my cursory research suggests that poverty and accompanying issues impact the quality of life in this community today.

Some historic animosity amongst German Lutheran population and a native Czech population seems to be a longtime part of the village culture. I've been able to witness videos of religious ceremonies online of what must be high-holy days in our old village. The last time I looked up Toperec online I watched a drone video of what they called the "Toporec Gypsy Encampment" and that one was difficult to watch, a grim looking spot. Not sure if it is a bipolar notion, or a normal one that I feel kinship to the people in this place. Even in as much as I would hate to inaccurately characterize the place or anyone else's home for that matter as not to offend. What I can say about the place with pleasure as evidenced by the all the big Svadba wedding celebrations videos is that it seems like there's a major tradition of great big wedding parties happening there with lots of people making lifetime memories in the little village. Not many places like it have that distinction.

So, there it was, finally revealed for the first time: the Stavnitski moniker and its roots. Digging through a random Eastern European ancestral travel guide, I came across Toporec's census going way, way back. The next aha moment was finding what at least for this amateur genealogist is the earliest original derivation of our name, from 1713–Styavniczky–which, for those who understand word origin, and who are maybe are little bit accustomed to an Eastern European accent, and who know us well enough, is precisely how we have always pronounced our updated version.

When one has a last name like ours, everyone assumes it's Polish. So, of course, when I was a kid, Polish jokes were all the rage, and all three of us "Stav" kids were the butt of them. Although we really had no idea what nationality we were, we were almost certain that we were not actually "Polacks." Still, we put up with it with good humor, even to the point where Betsy would, from time to time, be asked to share her mother-in-law's recipes for local Polish theme nights at local clubs and restaurants. This really made her laugh, especially because she was not a fan of traditional cabbage rolls and stuffed peppers, but she still lovingly prepared them for George once in a while, and she was a great cook. The only other clues were our holiday traditions from George's side. These included kielbasa with hard-boiled eggs and rye bread for Easter Sunday and what we called "Hunky Cookies" of soft dough folded at the ends filled with apricot or poppyseed at Christmas. That was the extent of our understanding of George's genealogy. You can imagine it was exciting learning after decades and decades, the source of our own history heretofore unknown to us. Hopefully, in the not to distant future, I will travel to Toporec and experience it.

George's childhood was no doubt a colorful one. George always described his childhood as very poor, but this may not really have been true. Because it was such a far cry and modest compared to what he had become accustomed to in his own household with Betsy and the more refined lifestyle passed on to our immediate family by his in-laws, perhaps he built up the illusion of his past as a kid who came up from the tough side of the tracks. George's family was happily working class and grateful for it. In Bridgeport they had lived in a "Hunktown" brownstone, with Great Grandma, Aunt Bessie and her girlfriend Frenchy, George's parents, and his little sister Barbara all cozy together. Later, George's much younger brother Kenny came. No doubt "Hunktown" would no longer be considered a proper name for a neighborhood, but that's what it was in those days, people didn't really think anything of it.

When George was a boy, like many enterprising immigrants, the women in the family in our case, Grandma Dominko, Aunt Bessie, and Frenchy, and George's mother owned and operated a small business. They ran a neighborhood bar and dining room and, during prohibition, a speakeasy in "Hunktown" called the Spruce Grill. Grandpa Stav worked part-time at the bar as well; they all pitched in. They prepared and served ethnic meals and had a live band with dancing on Saturday nights. The Spruce Grill also sponsored the Fairfield Dragons semi-pro football team. George's side of the family still sing the Dragons' fight song when they are drinking. It goes something like, "Ching-ling, ling, ling, ling! Who told you so? Ching-ling, ling, ling, ling! We told you so!"

George's stories of the years of shining shoes on the street corners of Bridgeport and at the bar are usually long and hilarious. Even better are the tales of his boyhood experiences as an altar boy. Pictures of George in his starched, pressed vestments with knickers, puffy sleeves, and bows holding chunky brass candlesticks are priceless. One can see him grow into his early teens in a progression of old sepia-tinted photos. We children would all groan when he started to go on about it, but Betsy never failed to provide a good hearty laugh at the altar boy stories.

In those days, if there was a funeral at Bridgeport's Holy Cross Parish, the altar boys apparently rode in the limousine jump-seats with the family from the church to the cemetery. After that, in addition to assisting the priest at the gravesite, they also helped the undertaker with the equipment used to lower the casket into the grave as the mourners watched. George never forgot those rides and often quoted his fellow passengers, the widows and other mourners in the limo as saying things like "I never did like that son-of-a bitch," or a fresh widow exclaiming, "I knew he cheated on me; I'm glad he's dead!" He'd then proceed with a description of the altar boys' excitement when they came across a distraught, sobbing babushka woman during funerals.

When it came time to lower the coffin, assisting the funeral director, the altar boys had control and could jerk the crank a little and jar the coffin as it was lowered and maybe even bring it up and down a bit to provoke more shrieks and tears. This made for gleeful retelling amongst the boys after the ceremonies back in the church sacristy.

Most of George's altar boy stories end with his grandmother or his mother, possibly both, barging briskly into the clergymen's office to give them a piece of their minds, reminding the clergy of the influence of their positions in the altar guild and the importance of their tithe to the church's coffers. No one could cross their precious Georgie! One priest, in particular, was known to be mean to the altar boys.

One afternoon late during Lent, George served the Stations of the Cross service alone. Although normally, two boys would assist the priest. At the right moment, George took position, struck a match, and lit the incense. It started to properly smolder and smoke in the vessel, but then he accidentally knocked it over and had to stomp it out during the service, rubbing permanent black marks into the church's carpet. This made the aforementioned priest awfully angry; he was bent on punishment.

Typically, after Mass, altar boys would kneel to receive the priest's blessing before heading off home or to school. This time, as punishment for the incense incident, George got his blessing, and then some! "Father, Son, Holy Spirit–Bam!" A right cross punch to the face from the angry priest. George went home saddened, feeling guilty, but desperate to keep it a secret. Like a hawk, Grandma Dominko quickly ascertained the source of George's pain, and of course, off she went to let the priest have it.

George's most prized time with his own father was rare opportunities to see the New York Giants play at the old Polo Grounds. He loved every minute of it and couldn't get enough of it. It became his childhood dream to play football one day with the New York Giants. By the time he was a teenager, if George wasn't at church or school, he could be found at the practice football field. He was a great long snapper, and in his spare time, he spent hour after hour snapping the ball at the proper distance between center and punter through a tire attached by a rope to the goalposts. He eventually became so talented that he never missed.

By the time he began playing high school football, it was also clear that George could hit like a Mack Truck. Even better, he had tremendous killer instincts and excellent quickness. Prodded by both teachers and coaches, George realized early that a college football scholarship was the best way for him to get an education that was beyond his family's means. To bolster both his academic standing and his football maturity, and with his coaches' support, he earned a one-year scholarship to Connecticut's prestigious boys' prep school, Cheshire Academy. That year changed his life forever. To this day, more than 65 years later, he claims it was the second-best thing that ever happened to him in his life aside from his marriage. As one of his children, hearing this was funny, expecting the next best events after marrying Betsy would be the days his kids were born.

George was athletically ready for major college football by his senior year in high school. His academic skills, however, were apparently not good enough for him to be successful at major colleges or universities. Cheshire Academy provided those skills, enabling him to compete both on the football field and in the classroom at schools across the country. To cover additional expenses, George worked in the prep school kitchens.

Cheshire's football schedule was primarily played against Ivy League freshman football teams. They lined up a lot against yearling football teams from Yale, Dartmouth, and the like. By the end of his only football season at Cheshire, with improved study skills and academic accomplishment, George had become one of the best blue-chip center and linebacker college football recruits in the nation.

His mother and little sister faithfully kept all the clippings and souvenirs of George's next few years. His primary targets were Penn, University of North Carolina at Chapel Hill, Dartmouth, University of Connecticut, Indiana, and Notre Dame. He garnered offers from all of them. He eventually chose to become a Carolina Tar Heel, heading south in the summer of 1953. He arrived to meet his two roommates, a gymnast, and a swimmer. He was randomly reunited with both fifty years later in their retirement.

CHAPTER 4

BOY INTERRUPTED

Now that we have some background, let's dive back into my life. To bring you up to speed, my first depression slowly sunk in through my freshman, sophomore, and junior years in college between 1982 and 1985. This emotional slumber signaled the real onset of my bipolar disease. Once again, I've reached a juncture where it's time to consider how much I am really willing to share. As I've suggested already, madness is not kind, and life isn't always polite. My parents' discretion was passed on to me. The subjects of family, any references to religion, politics, drugs and alcohol, and sex were well and properly prohibited, especially we would laugh at cocktail parties. Although I did promise at the outset that I would share some of my deepest secrets, there are still some things I'd much prefer to keep to myself. The truth is, I can't really write a meaningful memoir if I don't push through and publicly unburden myself. So, I will repeat, after a few deep breaths, in through the nose and out through the mouth and take a leap of faith.

My memory definitely has a "Rain Man" quality to it. Events, people and places, lyrics, some decent Shakespeare, and quite a bit of high school French are only some of the old data I can resurrect from the vault at just the right moment. Some people appreciate it. I know it bores others. Even when my vision was through the tinted blue lens of depression, I have always loved every minute spent with the people in our lives, so many of them, all of them great in my mind. Everyone who knows me well will tell you, I remember just about everything, I almost never forget.

Fascinating that with just a few clicks on my iPhone, I can pinpoint almost exactly the actual date of my first cognitive memories. A bit to my surprise, these were days just after my fifth birthday. In my mind's eye, I would have thought my earliest recollections would have been earlier than that, as early as age three or four. Now I realize, however, that any of my memories prior to age five are more like flashes before my eyes jarred by my mother's Kodak moments rather than real events.

The 1968 stop-gap animation Christmas television special "The Little Drummer Boy" premiered on NBC on December 19, 1968. The long thread that is my memory also premiered that night. My brother and sister and I were watching and listening to "Pa rump pa pum pum" on the edge of our seats on our big hotel room bed at the Imperial House Hotel South Dayton, during a family holiday trip from Oregon where George's career had taken us.

I found this Little Drummer Boy show on YouTube, and of course the memory of that visit came right back. There we are, the three of us inserting nickels or dimes into the bedside coin-op vending machine they used to have in hotels to make the bed shake and vibrate while we were watching Christmas specials on TV. This kind of useless stuff comes back into my consciousness from time to time. This happens a lot, one of the tenets of my bipolar brain.

On that plane trip from Oregon where George had been transferred in 1965 when I was two, back to Ohio, Betsy had us kids dressed to the nines. A crested blazer and bow tie for me, a suit, and a grown-up tie for my older brother, both of us in carefully shined leather shoes, and a perfectly pressed pinafore for our sister in her patent leather Mary Jane shoes. My parents laden with arms full of kids ages five, seven, and eight, along with fists full of luggage still would have been dressed as if they were going out for cocktails, mother in pearls and heels, and George suited up sporting a fedora. On the plane, we got little zippered goody bags sent back with a wave from the cockpit, including wings which airlines used to hand out to young passengers.

Grandma and Grandpa had just downsized from their spacious Georgian Colonial to a large three-bedroom sleek apartment-condominium; Grandma Connie's usual tricks with her designer gave it the look and feel of a New York City penthouse. She still had the same full-time help she had in the big house: Hazel in the kitchen and handy with a needle doubling just a bit as a lady's maid, and Wesley the butler, Grandpa's help, and occasional driver. They would live in the condo just one year before moving to Hilton Head.

During that visit, guests came in the evenings to my grandparents' apartment to spend time with George and Betsy, who were enjoying reunions with old friends. Us kids were impressed by the elevator. Guests' arrivals were first signaled by a buzzer and the sound of their voices on the intercom at the main entrance to the building, so we could look over the wide, awning-covered balcony and see who was coming below. Guests ascended in an elevator to our Grandparents' apartment on the top third floor. There, they were greeted by Wesley, dressed in a service tuxedo with a bow tie and white jacket. He would take their coats, drink orders, and adjourn, returning only minutes later with drinks on a doily covered silver tray. Depending on the formality of the occasion, Grandpa might appear in a silk smoking jacket and cummerbund, just to host friends and family for cocktails at home!

Even if it was just our family, Hazel would be in the kitchen and Wesley was there to wait on us at dinner. I still picture him, all smiles in his white coat and tie, carving the Christmas turkey on Grandma's elegant dining room table, furniture and dishes which I later inherited. The Christmas tree, which I'm sure Connie had decorated and delivered by a florist, was coated in heavy flocking. We watched with glee as

Wesley chucked it, stripped of decorations, off the back balcony, fluffy flakes of fake snow streaming in the air as it fell four floors beneath us onto the concrete service yard below. I vividly remember meeting my cousin John, age two, in a highchair in grandma's kitchen. My brother got a Baltimore Colts uniform for Christmas. We both got army uniforms, an awkward fashion trend for boys in those days, as the Vietnam war was in full swing. In the evenings it was back to the Imperial House South, which years later I learned had a popular nightclub called the "Boom Boom Room".

We would return to Oregon for the new year, 1969. We had such a wonderful time with all of the kids on our street. My brother and sister's activities were really my domain. My brother joined baseball and basketball teams coached by George and a buddy. My fiscally prudent parents seldom felt the need to hire babysitters, so I almost always got to tag along. Gymnasiums and little league ballparks were playgrounds full of friends for me. Betsy was a den mother for both Cub Scouts for my brother, and Girl Scouts for my sister. She became president of our elementary school PTA. I went to meetings, outings, sleepovers with all of the big kids. There were summer hikes and winter ski trips, as well as rodeos in the summertime, plus all that fun around by our neighbor's family pool. All of us Stavnitskis were having the time of our lives in the Pacific Northwest.

That's why it's so hard for me to reveal what happened to most certainly just in time for my long-term memory to start at four or five, just home from our happy Christmas trip to Ohio. By this time, I had already been experiencing sexual abuse with some regularity at the hands of at least three separate male predators in our Oregon neighborhood. Hard to tell, but best I can figure, it lasted for five years or more until we moved back to Ohio when I was turning 10. One perp was an infrequent babysitter from a nice family who lived across the street, with much older boys in high school and college.

He was the oldest of my three abusers, a guy between maybe 18-20. I know Betsy was fond of his mother. Another was a teenager who lived up the street, and finally another boy my own age who sadly perpetrated some bondage and sadomasochism on me, things that at that age that he could have learned from an adult. Implements used on me included backyard croquet equipment. Things I experienced had to be taught to these younger abusers from older men in the neighborhood. There must have been some pretty sick dark secrets in that neighborhood.

It's devastating to write this, for I know how much it will sadden family and friends if they read it, especially those who knew me then as a happy little boy, and who, like me, have such fond memories Oregon and this special time in our lives. It scares me too, because those close to us in that era will be able to identify those who are implicated here. I hope not. I have relegated these memories to the kinds of things that happened to lots of us as kids, good or bad. In those days, we were thrown in the way back of a station wagon on the metal surface without seatbelts and played with the popular impalement risk Yard Darts game. We survived.

A few years after we had moved back to Ohio and were settled in our new home, I was startled when the whole family whooped and hollered for me to come down from my bedroom to the family room to see something on TV. Everyone was gleefully glued to the set. Turns out my oldest perpetrator, the babysitter back in Oregon, was a contestant on the popular 70's network TV program "The Gong Show!" He was performing a comedy act with Warner Brothers cartoon character imitations. He quickly got the gong as well as the old vaudevillian style hook they used to drag bad acts off the stage. This was probably too much for me to process at perhaps 12 or 13 years old. It is perhaps one of my earliest life events that reminds all of us that real life can sometimes go beyond the imagination of fiction. We all get that sense from time to time when something really wild happens to us, and we think to ourselves, "You just can't make that up."

Despite the abuse, obviously, a sad episode in my life which I kept a solitary secret for nearly half a century, I really was a happy kid. I seem to have been able to compartmentalize it, and even through years of therapy and recovery from mood disorder in my 30's, and 40's, I never mentioned it, either to a confidant or to a professional. I didn't forget it. I just never gave it much thought. Sure, I was ashamed, but even now, I do not believe it is a source of my depression. It may, however, have had some significant bearing on my bipolar mind, for I never cognitively made the connection between the abuse and the fact that for the next half century afterwards, for almost my entire life, I flew solo. I definitely enjoyed plenty of great friendships throughout, but an intimate loving relationship or a proper romance was never in my wheelhouse. After sharing this secret, if this is ever published, I know many people whom I know and love who will simply think, "Well, that answers a lot of questions about Bob" Maybe this public airing of my age-old secret will simply fill in the blanks and make sense for many people.

CHAPTER 5

OUR CROWD

My brain chemistry must have changed at just about the same time my grandfather passed away in 1981, although his death definitely a milestone, it was not a trigger for any depression. As a boy and a young man my mood and state of mind were always happy and motivated. I had always been sensitive, but the feedback I had gotten all the way through my upbringing made me feel like a real winner.

My grades in high school were above average A's & B's. I could have done much better, a C would infuriate Betsy, but I was highly social and busy year-round with sports and jobs. There was not a lot of room for complaining. I had stacks of blue ribbons, MVP trophies, was co-captain on both swimming and wrestling teams, and enjoyed a successful high school football career. I even qualified twice with another buddy for the Ohio State Wrestling Championships, a rare feat for our preppy high school known instead for golf, tennis, field hockey, and forensics. George and Betsy made every meet, game, or match. With another mother, Betsy even earned an honorary varsity letter awarded for driving our high school wrestling team all over southwest Ohio. My name and even my picture were in the local papers a lot. I landed the leading role in our high school spring musical, "South Pacific;" the music from my rendition of "Some Enchanted Evening" in 1982 has followed me ever since. Then came the beginning of my excruciatingly long and still seemingly unending post-secondary academic career.

Our little hometown in Ohio is called Oakwood, this share is a bit too close to home as it further reveals my identity and delves a little deeper into our privacy. The truth is the wonderful folks from this town almost deserve their own chapter in my story. Oakwood is situated just south of Dayton, incorporated in 1908 and developed on higher ground especially after the Great Miami River Flood which devastated Dayton in 1913. Early neighborhood homes were designed to accommodate executives either from the thriving National Cash Register Company or from the automobile industry, as Dayton was somewhat of a developing mini-Detroit in those days. Oakwood's west side neighborhood consists of winding brick avenues lined with impressive full-on mansions, many with elaborate grounds designed by great architects of the 1920's and 30's from New York, Chicago, and elsewhere. There, architectural styles run the gamut: Tudor, Italianate, French Chateau, Gothic, Georgian, Victorian, to name just a few. Each is beautifully maintained. Oakwood's exclusive west side is centered around the Dayton Country Club golf course and is bordered by acres and acres of the wooded Hills and Dales Park. The park was designed by famed landscape architects from the Olmstead firm who designed New York's Central Park. Olmstead's vision for Dayton's Park was in the Adirondack style with sturdy stone picnic and civic shelters with fireplaces, scattered amongst riding trails.

All these old structures have been restored and are busy, with the exception that at the highest point in the park, standing sentinel is a singular, maybe three-story round stone castle turret, some called the witch's tower. When we were teens, it was still open to the public and we could walk up the winding staircase to an observation deck. A keen view of the moraine that my high school geology reminds me of the formation upon which the neighborhoods and towns adjacent to us along the Great Miami River developed. My understanding is where we lived and grew up was on the landmass on top of rubble that piled up at the end of the melted polar ice cap, which is why just a few miles east on I-70 or North on I-75 first time travelers can't believe how flat Ohio is, or how green it is driving for hours as far as the eye can see. Ohio was smashed flat and fertile on the outside edge of the ice age. Therein lies the origin for the moniker Moraine, a nearby suburb as well as for the namesake of the tawny Moraine Country Club nearby.

I'll stop right here to suggest this bipolar memory and rumination is probably a decent snapshot on how a bipolar mind can digress and how a bipolar memory serves. I indeed have a knack for recalling many detailed events stored deep in the vault of my past right on the spot and often with perfect timing. On the other hand, there are times my recollections might be slightly amiss, maybe a smidge out of chronological order, probably over time elaborated upon. I'm confident for the most part that my recall is close enough, at least for me. For example, the description of Ohio's topography I've given is definitely flawed, after all it is 45-year-old information from a seventh-grade quiz randomly triggered and whether or not I get it 100% right is OK with me. I feel a sense of illumination when my mind works in this way shedding light from the past on what I am experiencing in the moment. Often, I experience full circle moments in this way.

Here's the key to what I mean when I suggest the bipolar brain experiences the world in cool ways. In this case, my mind has taken me back to the top of the tower at Hills and Dales Park in Ohio. Even as I type, I can see that view crystal clear in my brain, almost photogenically. And to see it stretch for miles in the distance from above, since all we saw in Ohio most of the time were cornfields and soybeans, the view is pretty nice. I appreciate the memory, and happy that view fleetingly transported me to something I learned in the late 1970's and reminded me of two great teachers who fostered my interest in nature, neither of whom had crossed my mind in ages, both of whom as an adult I call friends.

Then, triggered describing the flat Ohio landscape I have just written about, I experienced the memory of more than one solo road trip on forever flat I-70 Eastbound in one of my dubious sets of wheels beyond Columbus closing in on Zanesville praying the corn and soybean fields would end soon while dodging orange cones for hours counting down the miles to the West Virginia border dying to get the hell out of Ohio. When these internal mental distractions happen, it even feels like a run on sentence in my own mind, but I try to take a minute to reflect on why I am thinking about whatever tangent that has taken hold and take a minute to make use of the moment. As I picture myself years ago, bored and anxious in my car on I-70, I think to myself, you've really come a long way since those days. My brain diverts quickly in this way. If I were to time it, the internal video of my junior high science class lessons, remembering my teachers, and the flashback to those '80's road trips through Ohio would come in at about 90 seconds. This minute and a half break my brain took from living in the moment was a good one. These interludes are not all happy or productive in this way. My batting average for successfully managing these is about .600. And then suddenly these thoughts pass, and I am generally back to the last paragraph at which I left off, as is the case here.

To take an unsuspecting visitor on a drive through the streets of Oakwood's west side is fun. Their jaws drop at the size and beauty of the homes, and right away they are perplexed by the display of concentrated old school wealth. It seems oddly juxtaposed alongside the much more modest city of Dayton. One would expect a neighborhood like this in the Hamptons, Boston, Chicago, but in the Rust Belt, it's unusual.

Oakwood's east side, where we grew up in what real estate agents refer to nowadays as the Golden Triangle, is not quite as impressive, but it still has its own elevated charm. Block after block of wide streets centered around tree-lined grassy boulevards create a park-like setting and a walking community. Here, there are smaller but still stately homes, like my grandparents' Georgian house, built in the 20's and 30's which are nestled amongst more discreetly sized family homes of the same era to accommodate Dayton's growing population of mainly upper-middle class families. This side of Oakwood is lined with big welcoming front porches featuring waving American flags and freshly mowed lawns, many with colorful displays of seasonal flowers. Most properties literally shine with pride of ownership.

Oakwood's east side neighborhood is centered around two elementary schools, the combined Junior and Senior High School building in the middle; and the old YMCA building which is now a city-owned multipurpose facility with a tennis center and community pool, which Betsy was on the board of for many years. Nearby, the private Virginia Hollinger Tennis Club has clay courts. Two quaint little shopping districts consist of barbershops, beauty salons, dress shops, banks, antique shops, doctors' offices, insurance agents, and the like. The busiest and most prominent of these limited commercial enterprises, and the foremost community gathering place is the originally humble but increasingly elegant Dorothy Lane Market. It's there that we all run into each other, catch up, maybe gossip a little and get some news while picking up groceries. After that, there's the ubiquitous Starbucks, and the popular Oakwood Club restaurant, a really great relaxed fine dining experience.

Oakwood's most prominent citizens to this day remain Orville and Wilbur Wright. The classic columned white neo-classic mansion the brothers built together is called Hawthorne Hill. It resembles a small version of the White House and stands sentinel just as a great historic American house should. It's nestled amongst other pristine estates just around the corner from the Oakwood City Hall, a unique long brick English Tudor styled municipal building with slate roofs. The nearby Wright Memorial Public Library is another gem of Tudor architecture.

And, while small in comparison to other fine school districts, Oakwood's City School District is absolutely top notch, due partially to Oakwood's notoriously high taxes. Even though graduating classes in our day averaged only around 150 students, test scores and other indices have almost always placed Oakwood High School at the top of the heap of Ohio's public schools. It has provided its students with a wonderful classical education. Involvement from the community had a lot to do with the success of the school system. The environment also inspired success.

Our two elementary school buildings look like university halls. Harman Elementary is an impressive brick Georgian affair fronted by tall white pillars, forming a classic colonnade, these days enclosing a sculpture garden. Smith Elementary School is another impressive Oakwood English Tudor which has its own formal front façade with intricate wrought iron arches supporting a slate roof. The combined Junior and Senior High buildings are even more impressive. Oakwood's largest English Tudor structure, the high school façade is topped by a sturdy slate roof-covered clock tower and looks almost like Hogwarts Castle from Harry Potter in miniature. The building sports-stained glass windows, a loft and an ornate working fireplace in the library, as well as a large formal auditorium with a proper theater lobby, large balcony, and voluminous arched ceilings framing a classic stage proscenium arch draped with heavy velvet curtains. The drinking fountains at either end of the senior hallway is of an art deco Italian floral motif and are priceless Rookwood Pottery creations. Even the high school football stadium adjacent to the junior high building was made of brick and designed to look like the embattlement wall of a Tudor castle complete with spiked wrought iron railings across the top ledge. This lofty environment gave, at least for me, the sense that we were learning in hallowed halls of higher education.

Another neighborhood favorite spot is situated at the base of the Wright Brothers Hawthorne Hill. Smith Memorial Gardens has long been known as one of Ohio's most beautiful small public gardens. Here weddings, small concerts called the Blankets Series, puppet shows, and even poetry readings take place. From here, a quick walk further down the hill on the old, bricked section of Oakwood Avenue winds into the wooded Elizabeth Gardens & Bird Sanctuary and babbling Houk Stream Park where locals walk in the forest with pets and Oakwood students enjoy as an outdoor laboratory for science classes, and likely use it as a place to sneak a smoke.

Still, as much as I enjoyed the town, it wasn't because there were big fancy houses and nice amenities. The best part was all of the people and families that called Oakwood home. The families in our town represented excellence in my eyes. So many nice intelligent, sophisticated, funny people that we knew for generations. We knew them so well, for so long, and shared so much fun with them as decades passed. I really aspired to end up like a lot of these people who inspired a lot of us just because of their presence.

After graduating from Oakwood High School and armed with everything my parents and grandparents could give me, I confidently headed off to Allegheny College in Meadville, Pennsylvania. Having been Big Robert's alma mater, as well as his fathers before him. I would become a third generation Allegheny Alligator. Our recently deceased Grandpa Allen was my benefactor, having set up full college trust funds for all five of his grandchildren. Betsy and George, he encouraged, would pay it forward and one day pay for my children's higher education. I was not oblivious to how fortunate this was, nor were my parents aware that the trust's loose arrangement would enable me to slide through the registrar and college bursar's office unsupervised for the next few years.

CHAPTER 6

DEPRESSION 101

My first predecessor as an Allegheny Alligator, my Great Grandfather, Dr. Tracy Thomas Allen is worth a few minutes here. Tracy graduated from Allegheny in 1899, the son of a banker from Fredonia, New York. There was a bank failure, causing Tracy's father, Henry Allen, the bank chairman, to lose everything. Family lore says this ancestor spent the rest of his life trying to pay back the citizens of Fredonia. Somehow, however, young Tracy was able to attend Allegheny, a small Pennsylvania Methodist College established in 1815, it was the first chartered college or university west of the Allegheny mountains. It was during my own time at Allegheny eighty years later, that I came across the documents of our Allen family ancestry and genealogy which became a lifelong interest.

Young Tracy Allen graduated from Allegheny at the turn of the twentieth century with a degree in education. He would marry his sweetheart from another Fredonia family and lead her and their two children, little Bob Allen, and his younger sister, our great aunt Margaret, all around Pennsylvania as a school principal and superintendent for numerous districts. In 1923 he was appointed President of East Stroudsburg State Teachers College in Pennsylvania's Pocono Mountains. He remained there as President for 17 years. He broke ground on a new grand President's Residence, an appropriate home for the head of such an institution, but way beyond what the discreet and humble Allen's would have chosen or expected for their own private home. They lived in it, 7000 square feet of grand subsidized housing, from 1930 for a decade through most of the great depression up to 1940. Tracy earned his doctorate in education from Columbia during his tenure at East Stroudsburg, and was proud to be referred to as Dr. Allen the rest of his life

Dr. & Mrs. Allen were devout teetotaling Methodists, but beyond that, one interesting pair. During the college's 1927 summer break, the two of them took a coast-to-coast driving tour. Wonderful, faded pictures on cardboard, with handy handwritten captions on the back, show them in an old 1920's open convertible touring coach at Pikes Peak, and in their black and white bathing suits with sleeves swimming in the Great Salt Lake. Dr. Allen became the District Governor of the Rotary Clubs in two states. He was a renowned sport fisherman, often traveling to Canada and Nova Scotia in search of the great catch, and was once pictured with a giant record-setting tuna easily more than three times his portly size.

They retired to St. Petersburg, Florida from autumn through spring, and summered in Asheville, North Carolina. In Florida, Great Grandpa devoted his time to volunteering as President of St. Pete's hi-rise Flori-de-Leon Condominium Association. Situated just a block from the beach, this was the very building in which Babe Ruth kept an apartment during spring training and is on the National Registry of historic sites.

Here, Grandpa honed his skill as a champion contract bridge player. I inherited his green leather bound embossed very old folk handed crafted family Bible cover; tucked away in it, amongst obituaries, funeral prayer cards, and telegrams expressing sympathy for various lost loved ones, are a pile of his bridge scoring sheets.

In full knowledge of a legacy set before me, and longing to be like my predecessors, it was my turn at Allegheny. I arrived with the expectation that life would come as easily to me as it always had. I figured I would go on to enjoy a career in politics, maybe get elected to Congress. Or perhaps my fallback position would be to go to graduate school, then practice law and live in a mansion on Oakwood's west side, the world my oyster. I just had to achieve well enough in school and relish the next four years, and I could make it happen. However, I had no idea that my first depression was beginning to sink in. It would be slow in coming over the next few years, an ebb and flow like the tide.

Although both Tracy Allen and Bob Allen had joined Phi Delta Theta at Allegheny. I did not receive a bid, even as a double legacy. Eager to be accepted, I joined another house, Delta Tau Delta. Generally, my freshman year living in the dormitory went OK, although I did quit the wrestling team which was a great disappointment to Betsy and George especially because I did it without telling them behind their backs.

The summer following my freshman year, I took an internship in Philadelphia, earning college credits and sharpening my political chops by working in the district office of a Democratic member of the US House of Representatives. I neglected to tell them I was a diehard Republican, but they never asked me. Every day that summer, I commuted an hour and a half by bus, train, and elevated lines from my apartment in Philadelphia's Germantown neighborhood to the Representative's office way across town in suburban Lansdowne.

At the Congressman's office, I answered phones, opened the mail, filled out forms on constituent complaints and requests, and arranged tours of the Capitol building and White House for constituents. My primary objective, the part of my internship upon which I would be graded, was to write the Congressman's position paper on women's issues and produce three issues of the office's monthly newsletter sent out to all households in the district. I wondered why, looking back, they had a 19-year-old guy write political pieces on women's issues. I must have done a great job though. I was given straight A's on all three components of my internship. I spent three days working in the Congressman's Washington, DC office, and fell in love with Capitol Hill.

Oddly, I have little recollection of after-hours carousing during that summer in Philadelphia. It certainly wouldn't have been unusual for a fraternity boy loose in a big city with money in his pockets. I can only surmise that a full day at a busy Congressional office, coupled with the three-hour commute, left me exhausted. There was also the fact that depression was beginning to loom over me. I was beginning to cope unconsciously self-isolating.

By the time I returned to Allegheny for my sophomore year to move into our "Delta Shelter" fraternity house a semester ahead, depression was in full swing. My ridiculous memory allows me decades later to still be able to recite the Delta Tau Delta Creed, secret words, handshakes, even the history of the brotherhood and its lore we were forced to memorize as pledges. As I grow older, I wonder if holding on to this kind of archival life data is helpful, as if my brain is filled to the brim, again distracting my ability to live in the moment.

I slept through most of the next 18 months or more. It didn't occur to me that I was sick. I just felt tired and bored. I was slowly and gradually flunking out. All of this, however, was unbeknownst to George and Betsy. They trusted my grades were fine; they always had been. I was a no-fail kind of kid. Financially, all I had to do was keep receipts for my expenditures and two or three times a year justify these with the trust officer for the account that Grandpa had given us; then, my college bank account was magically refilled. I even still had most of the money from my paper route and caddying, still carefully doled out to me as needed by Betsy.

I managed to get through my sophomore year English, Political Science, and humanities courses enough to squeak by. Still, most days, I would sleep until at least 2-3 in the afternoon. I was also experiencing something else new at the time. Some of my fraternity brothers didn't like me very much. As a matter of fact, out of maybe 50 guys living together, easily half of them thought I was an asshole.

Nothing like this had ever happened to me before. I'd been able to get along with just about anybody my whole life, but within a couple of years had developed into a polarizing figure. I was definitely lazy and could be arrogant. Furthermore, I was getting sloppy, ballooning up to 235 pounds, up 55 from my high school wrestling weight.

I made collect calls to Betsy and George maybe twice a month, always on Sundays. Less often, I would call Grandma at Hilton Head. My folks were beginning to feel the same way about me as half my fraternity brothers, for by this point, I was lying boldly to them about classes. I had them snowed and had them completely in the dark, but never gave it a second thought. Years later, it was actions like these which made me realize I was getting sick in those days. No one in his right mind from my family would behave the way I did.

Even though my fraternity brothers and my family plainly didn't like me as much as I did them, at this stage, I knew I could at least make them laugh. I still craved their favor and approval. This may have been my most important takeaway from these years. I'm not one to tell jokes, but with a long and specific memory, my humor is quick, occasionally sophisticated, and often spot on. My humor can be tricky; there's a learning curve, often even confusion before folks get to know when I'm serious or sarcastic. Once you figure me out, however, I can be hilarious. Good for most people, but only in small doses. This has gotten me into some trouble and out of a lot more of it over the years. I have been using humor to cover for my moods ever since.

I accomplished just a few interesting things in my remaining career at Allegheny, none of them academic. I wrote and sent twelve issues of our fraternity's Alpha chapter alumni newsletter called "The Choctaw

Pow Wow." I co-starred in a one night only, one act, student theater production of Neil Simon's "A Plaza Suite," playing the role made famous on film by Walter Matthau. As we rehearsed, I researched my Allegheny predecessors in their yearbooks at the college library. I wasn't really surprised to find both my Grandpa and my Great-Grandfather listed in the cast of productions on the very same stage in the 1890's and 1920's.

The day of the performance, George and Betsy left their jobs in Dayton at noon, hopped in the car, drove six hours to Pennsylvania, watched one act of "A Plaza Suite," kissed and hugged me in the lobby afterwards, then turned around and drove right back to Dayton that same night. As I was giving it my best Neil Simon bit, my fraternity brothers were slinging popcorn seeds, pennies, and other small bits and pieces on the stage to distract me. I pitied the funny, if awkward girl with whom I shared the stage, just the two of us. The play was clearly more important to her than it was to me, and my "brothers" could perhaps have demonstrated some class and compassion for her. This would be my last lifetime amateur theatrical performance.

My most gratifying college endeavor was to chair our annual fraternity fundraiser, a three day, 90-mile relay "Walk-a-Thon" between Meadville and Cleveland, begging for change at malls and grocery stores along the way. We raised as much as $16,000 each spring on those weekends, all for the compassionate Hawthorne Dominican nuns who ran a free-of-charge hospice facility for cancer patients in Parma, OH. Planning took several months and involved a mountain of logistics for the one fraternity brother who had to organize it every year.

Knowing I needed a vehicle for this effort, George and Betsy sent me back to school with Grandmother Connie's '78 golden yellow Mercury Cougar, which had snazzy back seat round opera windows, a creamy yellow half vinyl roof, spoked wheels, automatic opening and closing doors covering the head lamps. and a great cassette tape player. Man, did we ever have fun in that ride. Connie had earlier handed it down to Betsy. I put thousands of miles on this car with my fraternity brothers, our girlfriends, and Delt little sisters in tow.

When our walk-a-thon weekend rolled around, I was yelled at by nuns in two cities, but got hugs from lots of them in another. The first night of our walk was in sleepy Ashtabula, Ohio. There, probably 60 or more of us, slept on the floor in the gym at Mother of Sorrows Catholic Elementary School. Trinity Catholic High School in Cleveland was next. The final evening, we marched up State Road in Parma to the Holy Family Home and into the grateful arms of the Dominican Sisterhood. Both nights along the way, our college partying got out of hand; beer cans, trash, cigarette butts, and who knows what else had been found strewn all over both schools' properties. I was called into the principal's office at each. My only response was, "I'm sorry Sister; it won't happen again. God Bless."

My literal college swan song was a parents' weekend "Greek Sing" in the modest Methodist Allegheny College Chapel. Our Delt house seldom participated in Interfraternity Council events, so our appearance was unexpected. After a half dozen or so sweet Adeline performances by sororities, and some old school barbershop numbers from the other fraternity houses, we piled our rag tag group of Delt brothers. The entire audience immediately stood, for surprisingly, the pipe organ in the balcony sprang to life with the intro to "The Star-Spangled Banner." No other group had used the organ and its blaring shocked the crowd in the full chapel. After the anthem, our brother accompanist by design, raced loudly down from the choir loft. He then moved noisily through the center aisle to the grand piano in front of our obviously drunken group arranged like a choir on risers in front of the chapel's stained-glass window. Then, with a flourish of accompaniment on the piano, we broke into an altered barroom version of Frank Sinatra's "New York, New York," which I had earlier rewritten as a spoof to our college town called "Meadville! Meadville! The city that always sleeps," etc. Hilariously done right before college officials sitting in the front row.

We finished our performance with the more traditional "Delta Shelter" hymn. Instead of singing the middle verse, however, my brothers hummed the tune acapella while I made a quick off the cuff paragraph-long message of goodwill to our small college campus and gathered moms and dads. We brought down the house.

Two weeks later, my parents still in the dark, I went to the administration building, and with no other choice withdrew, officially flunking out. I called Betsy collect and asked her to come get me. She arrived by noon the next day, still in complete shock. Her son was dropping out from both her Dad's and Grandfather's alma mater. I moved out of the Delt House secretly like a phantom.

From a career standpoint, I never really overcame the missed opportunity to get my college degree. No doubt about it, that period was a turning point in my life which remains even today a profound lifetime game changer for a most likely to succeed kind of guy. Since then, I have never really felt like that same successful up and coming individual, aiming to be one of life's winners type ever again. My ambition and expectations remain diminished to this day.

Obviously, my increasingly thick depression was at the root of all this, but I don't recall feeling any excessively crushing sadness at the time, other than what one might expect when one's hopes and dreams come crashing down. Reliving that period brings tears to my eyes. Back then, all I really wanted to do was eat and sleep.

CHAPTER 7

BEST FOOT FORWARD

A proper recounting of my life would not be complete without the inevitable next uncomfortable reveal. I cringe to rain yet another family taboo topic. My use of drugs laid out for public consumption. My drug of choice is marijuana, plain old pot. Fortunately, as times have changed, marijuana has become downright acceptable. It's even available at retail outlets and is also considered a bona fide treatment for a number of medical issues. Still, I've yet to reside in a state where pot is legal for either medical or recreational use. No doubt, marijuana has changed me. I believe it enhances my ability to approach life as if I am looking at it through rose-colored glasses. That said, I would not recommend it to any other bipolar patient. That is up to them. I'll only say this makes sense for me.

In the early years of my therapy, as I discussed medications and prescriptions with my psychiatrists, I always made what I thought were obvious if veiled references to the fact that I smoked pot. I'm sure both counselors and doctors knew what I was driving at, to the extent of even recommending and prescribing medications known for the most part to be benign to the effects of marijuana. Occasionally, I've had to temper a prescription or had a happy manic reaction to something like the combination of Xanax, weed, and alcohol, but other than that happening just a few times, overall, I think pot and THC have helped me maintain a happy, balanced, creative, and frequently productive mindset through the highs and lows of life. Otherwise, the buzz I get from it keeps life interesting for me. These days everyone on my clinical and professional team are fully aware of my weed use, including how much I use, which I'll reluctantly share here might be a smidge on the far side of moderate.

I've tried to say good-bye to marijuana more than once. After all, where I live, it's an illegal narcotic; it pollutes my lungs, and is still not mainstream socially acceptable, especially now in my sixties. Ironically though, every time I ever seriously attempted to kick the pot habit, my closest friends and loved ones would gauge my behavior without it and encourage me to go find a fix. Over and over, throughout my adult life, different friends in different locales, in differing life circumstances, everyone seems to like me better when I am smoking. Perhaps it tempers my rather overwhelming personality in ways which make me more palatable to others. Like Forrest Gump, that's all I have to say about that for now.

I returned to George and Betsy's household in Dayton in shame, the first college dropout in our family. This was the beginning of about a 10-year period in which I knew my parents loved me, though I was also fully aware of the difference between like and love. Our relationship was filled with tension, making holidays and big family events really uncomfortable for all three of us and others for many years.

It became immediately obvious that we could not share the same home. I was quickly removed to a dreary one-bedroom apartment a few miles away and enrolled at Dayton's Wright State University. There, my folks hoped I could get back on my feet. I took a job in the men's department at the famous Rike's Department Store in downtown Dayton. Shortly thereafter, I was invited by my old high school football coach, a real local legend, to help coach the football team with two other good buddies from my class. Like me, they were also on "breaks" from their first college choices.

When that season started, I would not have guessed that the Oakwood football squad would end up having one of the best seasons in the history of our high school. Our preppy little team advanced to the Ohio State Championship Play-offs for the first time ever. The varsity team's success was coupled with an awkward, hysterical twist typical for me. While my buddies were varsity assistant coaches, I was to be the freshman head coach and also scout the varsity team's next opponent on Friday nights. As it turns out, both the varsity team and my freshman squad would experience nearly perfect seasons, but for completely different reasons! The varsity team posted a 12-1 record, only losing in the second round of the play-offs. My freshman team, on the other hand, went 0-6 without scoring even one point, nary a field goal or touchdown in their entire ninth grade season. They also hadn't put a point on the scoreboard during their entire junior high football careers.

That freshman team deserved a lot of credit. It had to take a lot of guts for those guys to keep their heads up, having been skunked three seasons in a row, and good for the cheerleaders and parents who trudged the far ends of southwest Ohio, faithfully rooting for them and kindly consoling them one loss after another. Despite the fact that major depression was unfolding during that season, I can't deny that it was a fun experience. I realize that I missed one recurring lifetime cue from these years, in part from the old school Iowa Test of Basic Skills we took every year. Almost every time the tests included occupational propensities; my result would inevitably indicate my most successful career path would be in education.

Perhaps I should have been a teacher. After all, I come from a decent line of educators, my great-grandfather a university president and my great-uncle the Dean of Men at Florida State in the 1950's and 60's. Although, to be thoroughly honest with myself, even I would probably find the idea of a teacher-coach with a drug habit distasteful, even if it is only weed. Imagine how parents would feel if they knew one of their kid's coaches or teachers was self-medicating with narcotics.

Always a salesman at heart, a skill handed down to me by George, I really excelled in retail sales at my part-time job in the men's department at Rike's. The environment of a crowded store was invigorating for me, and the management team was great. Things were also sailing smoothly in Wright State's classrooms. I continued to focus on the easy humanities classes, managing a B+ average. Within a year my progress was such that George and Betsy were willing to entertain a second shot of college away from home. I had acquired a valuable tool from my parents which has continued to sustain me all my life: I could perform in public, hiding my true feelings while appearing to be nothing other than happy, motivated, and successfully moving forward. I used that skill really successfully then, but no doubt about it, I was not at all well. It's a skill I recommend, as this willingness and ability to perform, indeed, to shine and fake it 'til you make it in public does wonders for a dull, broken spirit when one is alone.

CHAPTER 8

A CAPTIOL DEPRESSION

Sick or well, I was definitely ready to get hell away from my parent's control and out of Dayton, Ohio, and was still planning to do it on the dole of family generosity. Before I was allowed, they made me consult with two people: our wonderful parish priest, and a therapist to determine if there were any obstacles with drugs and alcohol that would upend my ability to be successful away from home again. Boy, did we ever totally miss the boat at that point!

After a couple of therapy sessions, and the completion of an old school scantron fill-in personality assessment test, we were told that I needed to be aware of addictive tendencies. That was it! In retrospect, I was already three years into a bipolar career at this point, but there was no hint of it as a result of my first foray into the mental health system. Our wonderful priest, blessed my sendoff, even set me up with a place to live in Washington, DC, where I was headed off to attend American University.

It had been arranged that I would live in the basement of a retired elderly Washington, DC lawyer by the name of Joe Keller, who had grown up in Oakwood. He lived close to both American University and the National Cathedral in Northwest Washington. It was a wonderful neighborhood, but I only stayed for two nights. I was creeped out by the fact that also sharing another room in the basement were two Filipino boys about my age. I couldn't decide whether they were roommates, students, houseboys, or what was really happening there. I quickly retreated, never even thanked the man, packed up my car and left. Years later a headline in the Dayton Daily News revealed that Joseph Keller had been counsel to Presidents from FDR through Kennedy and had donated millions of dollars to build the new law school at the University of Dayton. My manners definitely failed me on that one.

For a few days after I left the Keller residence, I explored Washington. Right away, I found a great furnished basement apartment in a brownstone on Park Road Northwest. It was adjacent to the colorful, primarily Hispanic Adams Morgan neighborhood, and close to Rock Creek Park and the National Zoo. It was a fantastic situation for me, the only drawback was no off-street parking for the car, which was a 1983 Chevy Malibu Wagon, my parents bought used for me with the knowledge that I would at least have dependable transportation, though it was not exactly a sporty choice for a 20-year-old.

Days afterward, I appeared at the Congressional office where I had interned while at Allegheny in Philadelphia and was brought on immediately as an unpaid intern. As far as I was concerned, this was no problem, as my lifestyle was supported by the educational trust set up by my grandfather. The longtime Congressman was in the final push of a 1986 U. S. Senate Campaign against Arlen Specter. This was exciting stuff. Every day, I donned a tie and headed from my little furnished basement apartment to the US Capital and Rayburn House Office Building. As far as both my family and I were concerned, I was back on track, in politics at a young age, and really in the thick of things. Yet, I was unknowingly still spiraling downward into depression. I never did enroll in American University. There was no way. It was a huge, dishonorable lie. I'll rationalize years later; I really did not have enough in me to be a part of Congress and go to school at the same time.

For a few months, I had a bird's eye view on national politics. I traversed the halls and tunnels of the Capitol building carrying out lots of tasks, most menial, some important. I lunched on Capitol Hill, hung out in the Library of Congress. I got to take the train back to Philadelphia to work at the Congressman's Senate Campaign headquarters. We were in lockdown when Corazon Aquino came from the Philippines and spoke before a joint session of Congress. I wandered into the House Gallery one afternoon and just happened to sit in on and witness Tip O'Neil's famous "Man of the House" speech upon his retirement. I made deliveries to the Senate Office Buildings, walking into places like Ted Kennedy's office, greeted with familiarity no questions asked. I could hardly believe it.

I opened and sorted all Congressman's mail. One day a package arrived from none other than Barbra Streisand! In it was a floral tin box with silk lining which held a cassette tape with a recorded invitation from Barbara herself to "... Dinner and a concert at my ranch." The $5,000 a couple fundraiser for the Democratic National Senatorial Campaign Committee still gets played as Streisand's "One Voice" live concert album released a year later.

The November election rolled around. Unfortunately, the Congressman lost. Arlen Specter would enjoy a generation in the Senate instead. I was out of my unpaid job and not eager to find another one. I was a Republican after all, and none of them seemed to need interns. By now, my parents had figured out I still hadn't enrolled in school. On top of that, I had racked up hundreds of dollars in unpaid parking tickets near my apartment and at parking meters all around the Capitol. Paying up to get the boot removed from the Malibu had become a habit. I told my folks I had a lead on a job on Gary Hart's campaign for President. This was partly true, but never came to fruition. Needless to say, Betsy and George quickly cut me off. Their emotional baggage becoming heavier and heavier. It was time to let me go.

Through the Washington Post classifieds, I found a job making $13,320 a year in the management training program at Household Finance Corporation, also known as HFC, which provided small personal loans to consumers. Once again, I donned a tie and headed from my basement apartment in the wagon around the Capitol Beltway to the HFC branch office in New Carrollton, Maryland. This was definitely a far cry from the environment on Capitol Hill. I hated New Carrollton and Prince George's County, an environment that was not good for my mood. I made barely enough money to cover rent, utilities, gas, and grocery bills. My needs were meager as work was all I had energy for. I rarely went out and had only two friends from my HFC office. The inevitable isolation that comes with depression became a part of my life. In my off hours, I became somewhat of a hermit. I went to work, ate, slept, and watched TV. By this time, I was in full-on depression without knowing it. I would continue to be for years to come. It was a long, very slow burn.

When the home in which my basement apartment was situated was sold, I lost my lease. Fortunately, a girl who'd been a classmate at Oakwood was living in Alexandria. She and her roommate were looking for a third roommate to share a townhouse in Northern Virginia. I would fit the bill, although it would be a few weeks before we could move in.

In the meantime, a girl from my sister's class at Oakwood let me crash for a couple of weeks at her apartment with her other two roommates in Gaithersburg, MD. One evening while the three girls were out, I decided to rent the movie, "St. Elmo's Fire," while doing laundry. After a while, one of the roommates, an absolutely beautiful girl, arrived home. "I moved your laundry into the dryer," I told her. Within seconds, the worst shrieks I've ever heard came from that laundry room. Unfortunately, her cat had snuggled in the dryer before I had moved the clothes into it. I had run a full permanent-press cycle with the cat in it, never hearing its cries over the movie. As she ran screaming into the parking lot of a busy Gaithersburg complex, I reached in and got the cat out of the warm dryer. The poor thing looked like a petrified Puma Shoe logo splayed out as if running to catch up with the spinning dryer. Just horrible. The continued cries and screams from the enraged girl whose cat I had accidentally killed alarmed and confused the neighbors who assumed a domestic dispute had occurred. Within minutes, police cars were all over the parking lot. All kinds of people were yelling and screaming at me. Needless to say, my move to Northern Virginia was expedited.

We had a memorable year as roommates. Our third roommate, however, could not stand me. Again, I was learning that I could be a polarizing figure. She was an American Airlines flight attendant and at the time was dating a secret service agent in detail at the White House. I realize now my personality was beginning to take leave of me in these years. Despite that, for that year I managed to share an apartment with two beautiful women.

My job at HFC progressed well enough, although the work was boring and beneath my capabilities. Within a couple of years, I was earning the paltry yet increased sum of $16,000. I had finally fallen way behind my friends in Ohio who were pursuing more successful and lucrative careers. Many were even heading down the aisle. This was not helping my self-esteem.

When HFC's operations were consolidated, I wound up in a branch in Clinton, Maryland that had been converted into a debt collection office. Days were spent calling people who should not have been extended credit in the first place, harping on them about late payments. For nearly two years, I became a professional bill collector. HFC district managers had gotten tired of so many loans being written off in bankruptcy court, so I was also assigned to attend bankruptcy hearings and object to filings when we had collateral. It was a futile job.

Still, off I went to courthouses in Rockville, MD, Alexandria, VA, and the District of Columbia to annoy judges in all three cities. I put a lot of miles around the Beltway in that 1983 Malibu wagon. It wouldn't be long before I drove it into the ground.

My depression was worsening, but I still managed to make friends with the group from the HFC collection office. We ate lunch together and often went for drinks after work. I was beginning to get pretty good and fat. Fortunately, the HFC experience would soon come to an end, as my new friends were into cocaine and were plying me with it. For a few short months, I would contribute as we pooled our money to buy an eight ball and snort it, usually at a nearby park after work or on weekends. It's one addictive high, and I was lucky to realize right away that cocaine is not for me. I could, however, get pot from them.

When HFC built their central collection and corporate offices in Chesapeake, Virginia, we were all offered relocation packages. Instead, I found a new job in collections at the Pentagon Federal Credit Union in a beautiful office building right on the banks of the Potomac River on the outskirts of Old Town Alexandria. The family could all save a little face in Ohio, vaguely explaining that I was working at the Pentagon, which really, I was not.

When the lease with the girls ended, I found new roommates through the Washington Post in a house a mere five-minute walk from the Pentagon office. Here, for the first time, I managed a great living beyond my means. The Watergate of Old Town complex we lived in had amazing grounds, formal gardens, koi ponds, and underground parking. They were relatively new townhomes, a stone's throw from the banks of the Potomac River. For a year, I shared the place with an insurance salesman and a couple of in and out guys, random roommates who failed to last. To this day, Old Town Alexandria is one of my favorite places, one of the most charming, quaint, sophisticated places I have ever lived.

When my insurance salesman roommate purchased a 17th floor hi-rise condominium in the Skyline complex in Alexandria. I moved in as well, so I was back to commuting. While living in Old Town and at Skyline in 1988 and 1989, it seemed to a certain extent as if my life was trending back on the rebound, although the bar had been set much lower for me in life. I was 25 years old, but I was not coming close to what I thought my life was going to be like at that age. I was also beginning to realize that my long-term prospects were not improving. I could never figure out why. I felt in my heart I had everything I needed to succeed, but nothing came easily for me anymore. It had become almost the norm, and I wasn't going to make it big, after all. How sad this was for me, not measuring up right out of the gate. I was biding my time, going nowhere. The only solace was that I was living in a city I loved.

While at HFC I connected with George's younger sister, my Aunt Barbara, and her family. Uncle Bing was the station manager for US AIRWAYS at Washington's National Airport. In those days before the TSA, I stopped in at the terminal and barged into his office, introducing myself as his long-lost nephew. We've been extremely close ever since.

They lived an hour south of Washington in rural Stafford, Virginia, in a stately white farmhouse built in 1888 with tall two-story columns over a great covered front porch at the end of a long sweeping drive that curved up a small hill as you approached the property. Behind the house, on 88 wooded acres were barns filled to the rafters with all kinds of old stuff. There was furniture, motors, broken down MG's and BMW's, boats, farm equipment, a school bus, lots of old signs, stacks and crates of miscellaneous auto parts, and more tools than I had ever seen any one person own. In his spare time away from the airport, Uncle Bing was an auction enthusiast, a dedicated picker. He's one of those guys who can buy, repair, or refurbish, and manage a decent profit on just about anything you can imagine. Aunt Barbara, at the time a successful real estate agent, was and is, one of the most relaxed, easy-to-be-around women I've ever met. Like everyone in George's family she'd been raised Catholic. She spoke frankly, usually reserving judgment, although her filter has ebbed as she's aged. Their two sons, my cousins, whom I had only met twice fleetingly in our childhoods, instantly became like brothers to me.

Other than our mutual loved ones, I shared almost nothing in common with these guys. Our toolbox at home in Ohio was the Yellow Pages, but my gearhead cousins could build, fix, or repair anything. Their heads were constantly under the hoods of cars, an activity that bored me to tears. Still, we could not have had more fun together. They would take me out in fields and shoot guns, go fishing, or we would listen to hard core rock and roll and party with their buddies in barns, in creek beds and in the woods. For a little while there, I had friends and active friendships.

By the time I moved to the Skyline condo, Uncle Bing had retired from the airline to launch his picking business full-time. He opened a small antique thrift store serving Stafford and Fredericksburg. The yard was full of old farm equipment, cement lawn furniture, all kinds of junk in my mind. The shop itself, an old farmhouse that was practically falling down, was chock full of a collection of broken-down antiques, plastic flowers, glassware, comic books, and loads and loads of other junk. I could hardly believe people would pay money for any of this, but Uncle Bing seemed to rake it in with this little operation.

On Friday evenings, I would leave my job as a bill collector and head south, fighting Washington's rush hour traffic in the Malibu, and head to the farm for the weekend. On Saturdays, while my uncle was at auctions in country hamlets all over Northern Virginia and Southern Maryland, I would man his store. Aptly named 'Country Bargains," it was a real slice of Americana. There were many regular customers, most of them real Virginia country types. Many of them had Confederate flags and gun racks in the windows of their pick-up trucks.

Since I had little idea of the actual value of a majority of the merchandise, I needed some coaching from Uncle Bing on big-ticket items. As a result, many of our customers had no trouble talking me down in price. He was frequently annoyed as I recounted the day's sales. Most of the time I managed a reasonable profit, but sometimes I'd been swindled, taken for a sucker. The worst of my deals involved selling a decent baseball card collection for pennies on the dollar. We would laugh at all of this, drinking cheap beer together back at the farm, then Sunday afternoon I'd head back north up I-95 to my real life in Alexandria.

For about a year, these weekends were a great relief from my mundane workday job, as well as living, working, and commuting in an overpopulated international city. My depression continued to take hold, so I really appreciated the unconditional acceptance of these wonderful relatives. There was no emotional baggage in these relationships. Telephone calls to and from home in Ohio with George and Betsy had all but ceased; my relationship with my immediate family was on the rocks. My living situation was getting dicey, my personality was tanking, and I'm sure I was not much fun to live with. Alberto the insurance salesman roommate, who was now also my landlord, had a fiery Puerto Rican temper, and could be demeaning. As time progressed, and I continued to ignore the warning light indicators the which was becoming a hazzard.

I was unaware my moods were affected one way or another. How I felt just was. In those years, my mood was more a lack of any kind of emotion whether it be happiness, sadness, sympathy, or empathy. I knew I wasn't usually particularly happy, but that didn't really bother me. Surrounded by the right people, I could still have a great time. Generally, though, life was beginning to feel like an endless string of long days staring at a blank piece of paper. Malaise and boredom were beginning to impact my ability to get my work done properly in the collections department at the Pentagon Federal Credit Union.

Cognitive brain functions were failing me. I would transpose dates or enter numbers wrong on my collection activity logs. My mind wandered. I had trouble making decisions. Finally, I found myself, always a talkative and engaged guy, with nothing left to say. No humor or wit. Not even sarcasm. This became obvious to me and to my business associates during smoke breaks. Normally I was full of life, eager to catch up, hear the latest. No longer. I would just stand there in silence, smoking and staring off into the distance, only nodding occasionally to my co-workers. My temperament had evolved into something of a slight daze.

It was the lack of brakes, their major grinding, and fear of being unable to stop the car that finally made me get rid of the faithful Malibu. I replaced it with a new red Mitsubishi Eagle 2 door hatchback. At 6 ft 2", it was ridiculously small for me, but it was all I could afford given the fact that I was only up to earning $ 22,000 a year at this point. My cousins on the farm blew me major flack about that car, which did not even come with air conditioning.

Regardless of the tension, my parents insisted I come home to Ohio for Christmas every year. Besides, I wanted to be with my family for the holidays. In my daze of depression, I drove home to Ohio in my new little hatchback to check out Betsy and George's new home. They had moved to Oakwood's westside after all, renovating and expanding a rambling ranch on the sixth fairway of the Dayton Country Club golf course. A great spot.

Following a long weekend of soul searching and tearful conversations, George and Betsy helped me realize that it was time to wrap up my Washington DC experience, put a bow on it, as George would say, and move back to Ohio. We all agreed I had connections, better prospects, and better support in Ohio for putting my life on track.

CHAPTER 9

A LIGHT BULB

Fast forward six years, to the summer of 1996. I am the landlord at my "slum" apartment building in Oakwood, making my curbside garden grow. I'd rebounded from a couple of job losses and was performing well in my security job. I had just won a national sales award, had joined both the country club and the Rotary Club, and enjoyed volunteering at the Chamber of Commerce. I was saving face again. "Faking it 'til I could make it," which had become a personal credo. This skill indeed eventually allowed me to experience actual creative successes in my life from time to time, however fleeting.

After nearly fifteen years of jumpstarts in life, and subsequent setbacks and disappointments, I had finally hit rock bottom depression. It was my boss, anxious to make his sales goals in the security business who called me out to lunch. He came to my rescue, and triggered the next level of my madness, all in the same conversation. We sat across the table at a local Greek restaurant not far from where our office was located and most of our business was conducted. His side of the conversation went something like this: "What the hell is wrong with you?" and "Pull your shit together, or you're going to lose your job!"

He was a nice guy, I know he cared about me, needed me to be successful, and hoped he could be helpful. I'm not sure if we talked about depression and cannot remember if he specifically recommended professional help, but eventually that was the result. Following this lunch, or just a few days later, the next memory of my spiral is the first moment of epiphany on my journey.

Taking myself back into my own head in the 1990's makes me feel sad. Looking back into a looking glass at my most very depressed self, the images that come to mind are dim, foggy, misty, and gray. There are also images of very sunny beautiful days one after the other, gorgeous days that for years I let go of in a hazy, sleepy stupor. It would be interesting to have friends and family who knew me then talk about what they saw, what I was like, what I did that I don't remember. What they thought and how it made them feel. I wonder how different their memories would be from mine.

My epiphany came at our favorite local bookstore, one of the first local mega-bookstores. It was a nice place to look around while running errands and to pick up gifts. I enjoy classic literature, a good bestseller, and sometimes a biography. I suspect I was looking in these aisles when I was compelled to check out the psychology section, perhaps looking for clues to my mood. I was lucky, and perhaps God had a hand in it, but the first book I pulled off the shelf and opened was to a page that included a clinical definition of depression. As I read, a light bulb went off. That's me. I'm depressed, no doubt about it.

I had good insurance and within days took the right next step and contacted my workplace Employee Assistance Program. I was sent first to a counselor, which I've learned over the years is standard operating procedure in these instances. After two appointments with a therapist, I landed in the office of a well-respected, highly recommended psychiatrist. He was a brusque guy in perhaps his late fifties. He was burly, balding, graying. Without much consideration he prescribed 20 milligrams of Prozac.

I took my first dose on Halloween. In less than thirty days, I ramped up to my first manic phase. My lens on life went from blue to psychedelic for the first time in a flash. By Thanksgiving, I was experiencing some delusions of grandeur and terribly pressured speech. Almost no one could get a word in edgewise with me. By mid-December, I no longer needed sleep.

It was totally out of character when I traded my car which I had recently upgraded to a new Honda Accord, for a pickup truck. Next, ignoring my parents' reservations, I started renovating my apartment building. In my unit, new carpet, paint, and who knows what else. The old place was really getting worthy of the name slum. I shelled out $ 30,000 to my down and out friends who were carpet layers and painters. My needy friends were taking advantage of me in my manic phase; things were spinning out of control.

As I write this, I've realized my highest level of psychosis was actually a garden variety manic episode. In the old days, most people would describe it simply as a nervous breakdown. With all that I have shared so far, even considering my own anticipation as I reveal what it feels like to lose your mind, it's something of an anti-climax, but I assure you the plot thickens as time passes.

I spent the month of December speeding as fast as I could in almost every way. Always a real grandpa behind the wheel, often driving under posted speeds, I was hauling ass up and down highways in my sales territory in that pickup. I was only a few key contracts away from another sales award, plus a nice bonus if I beat out the other two very competitive sales executives in our office. With a New Year's Eve sales year-end deadline looming, I was zooming through appointments, making deals, collecting signatures, getting it done, as one of my favorite coaches would say "quickly, quickly, quickly."

I was also pushing for a self-imposed Christmas deadline on my apartment renovations. I was making manic purchases in my mind thinking I was nearly finished, but the place was a train wreck. On one excursion to Home Depot, I managed to fill seven shopping carts pulling them along myself like train cars. I managed to hide this from a woman from the Rotary Club I ran into. "Bob, Are you OK?" She asked. "You look strung out!" I was living in a terrible environment both for me and my poor little dog Chipper with ripped up carpet, half painted walls, and sawhorses with paint cans and equipment strewn around my place. God Love that dog; he still leapt joyfully into my arms every time I came through the door and cried for a good while when I left for work. I was definitely not OK.

It was obvious to me and others that something was very wrong with both my medication and the resulting behavior. But like every other maniac, the feeling was fantastic. I loved it. I was determined to make it to the New Year at work. I had planned a vacation by myself to my grandparent's house on Hilton Head, where I could relax and think about making a change on the Prozac. I had already asked for the time off. I figured I could shake off whatever I was experiencing with a trip to the beach.

Finally, hours before the year-end deadline, I rushed back to the office to turn in a sale from a speedometer manufacturer in Dayton. Indeed, it appeared I was going to outpace the other members of our sales team and land in the coveted number one spot. I had the paperwork in hand and was called into the boss's office while catching a quick smoke with other associates. The speedometer company owner had called him and told the boss that I was "on" something and to please not send me around again. I was fired on the spot.

I went home to the slum probably in shock, but maniacally unphased. I had double booked appointments there that evening with an architect and also my stockbroker, a long-time buddy from school. They arrived at the same time. In my mind, the architect would show me how to re-style the old place, while my broker would show me how to pay for it. I expect these two nice guys wondered what the hell was going on. I was definitely crazed. Fortunately, George arrived and relieved these guys of my company. My boss had called George and Betsy and had told them that I was on drugs or that something else was very wrong with me, and that I had been axed from the company.

I'm not sure how I got there, but I found myself at my parents' kitchen table after a shower, in a pair of George's pajamas. Betsy, in nurse mode, was on the phone with a psychiatrist friend, one of George's golf partners. In the 1950's his wife and Betsy would walk to Oakwood Junior High together. Later, I was on the swim team at the country club with his children. It was one of those wonderful types of cross-generational family friendships we enjoyed and could call on in need.

With this going on, I was highly agitated. I yelled at Betsy when she put out a dinner of chicken broth for me, angered that she was feeding me as if I was some kind of hospital patient. She sent me to her guest bedroom, hoping I might sleep it off as they weighed options. I quickly locked the door behind me, popped a screen, and slipped out the window. I walked 2 miles on the brick roads of Oakwood's westside in bare feet wearing my father's pajamas in the midst of snow flurries, back to my slum in my neighborhood on the grid.

It was not long before my absence was noted. With help from my friend Pam, whom George had called in for back-up, I was delivered from my place to the emergency room at Kettering Memorial Hospital. I was a disturbance in their busy ER. Fortunately, I was quickly admitted, but from my experience in the security business, I was also fully aware that I had been sent behind the locked doors of an access-controlled psychiatric ward. "Holy Shit!" I thought. I had not expected this.

The hospital's attending psychiatrist saw me late that same night. It was my very own shrink, the curmudgeonly guy who had prescribed Prozac that had put me in there in the first place. "Who is your psychiatrist," he asked. I was completely incredulous. "You are. You're treating me, you asshole!" Still not a glint of recognition from him. This would be the first of many awkward moments with psychiatrists. A few years later, I read in the newspaper that this doctor would be stripped of his medical credentials. He was a total narcissist. I never saw him again.

I spent the next few days in lockdown, medicated and coming off my manic high. I attended group therapy twice a day, although I was the only "mental" patient in the circle. Later, I would realize that this would be a trend, as those of us with bad brain chemistry and mental health issues are often lumped in with alcoholics and drug addicts.

I made one very bad rookie mistake when I was admitted by refusing to permit my parents access to any of my medical information. Instead, I named Betsy's sister, my Aunt Nancy, who lived an hour away. She volunteered in the rehab unit at Cincinnati's Christ Hospital.

Advice for anyone who finds themselves in my shoes. When you're out of your mind in the hospital and have to sign off on caregivers, allow those who love you to help you. Shutting those loved ones out is an easy, even instinctive choice because you are likely angry at them and projecting your problems onto them, but not having them on board with your treatment can cripple your chances of success, however angry or estranged you might be.

After 4 days in the psychiatric ward, and more than anything wanting to go home and be left alone with my dog Chipper, I was paid a visit by my family doctor. At the time, he was also the Oakwood football team sideline physician and a cool guy. I think against his better judgment, he agreed to discharge me. Aunt Nancy arrived as this was happening. She took me aside and told me that I'd had a nervous breakdown, that it was no big deal and that was it. I was sent home with no actual diagnosis. To be honest, it didn't occur to me to ask. The billing office made me settle my account prior to discharge. Nancy later told me that the clerks had been mean to me. Before I knew it, I was home, back at the slum, which Betsy and George had cleaned up and set the apartment straight for me, including several huge cartons of laundered clothing they had found strewn all over the place and had sent to the laundromat while I was in the hospital.

Naturally, I was back into the weed immediately, which did not sit well with the medications I had been prescribed. After two days trying to sleep off everything I had just experienced, my condition worsened. It felt like anxiety kicking into nauseous bed spins like Mel Brooks in the movie "High Anxiety." I couldn't shake it, and knew I was not going to get better. While I was in Kettering Hospital, George had somehow managed to reverse the deal with the car dealer, so my Honda was back in the driveway in place of the pickup. I got in it and drove myself to St. Elizabeth's Hospital in downtown Dayton. I had myself admitted there, knowing more about what to expect and hoping for the best. It was one of the luckiest and best choices of my life.

I spent three nights at St. Elizabeth's, then was released home to attend their three-week partial hospital outpatient mental health program. I would arrive at the hospital at 8:00 a.m. for a blood test and a healthy breakfast, go through classes, enjoy a decent lunch in the hospital cafeteria followed by two more hours of classroom and therapy, then home by 3:00 p.m. Again, I was the only psychiatric patient in a group of alcoholics and drug addicts. This time, it worked for me. When the group therapy turned to the Alcoholics and Narcotics Anonymous programming, I was lucky to be given private therapy sessions, maybe with my weed habit I should have hung in with the group.

The latter half of week two arrived, and with it the inevitable family group session with George and Betsy. I had relented on the release of information to my parents. My psychiatrist this time was a portly, jovial, bearded gentleman in his sixties. He was primarily a court-appointed child psychiatrist who supplemented his practice in St. Elizabeth's "Stress Care Center" where my outpatient program was held. "Bob is Bipolar." He told us. "Are you certain, Doctor?" Betsy asked. "Absolutely no doubt in my mind," he replied. From that moment on there has never once been any doubt in my mind either.

Hearing for the first time that you have a mental illness, that it has a name, that it is bad, and that you're bona-fide crazy, is a strange thing. It turned my stomach and my mind on end, but I owned it from the moment the words left the doctor's mouth. With the progression of my life, a diagnosis of bipolar disorder made complete sense to me.

I was prescribed a cocktail of five drugs right out of the chute: Lithium (the gold standard); then a lowered dose of Prozac to boost my mood; Depakote to moderate it; Ativan for stress; and finally, Ambien for sleep. In the first sessions with my new doctor, I asserted that I would hope to wean myself off some of these medicines, and that I was not going to let a mental health problem ruin my life. Simple as that. Of course, it would never be as easy as all that, but I believed I could do it, and I think more than anything this positive mental attitude made the difference. Meanwhile, I concentrated on getting better, and at her request, gave my Ambien pills to my mother who was up all night worrying about me.

I learned a tremendous amount during those three weeks at St. E's Stress Care Center. Most important was to forgive the people upon whom I projected my problems, my parents, and Betsy in particular. Clearly, their influence on me could never have resulted in harm, although at the time I was sure they were responsible for just about everything that had gone wrong in my life. I loved them, but also resented them enormously. Dismissing this narrative was liberating for all three of us, but it was easier for me than it was for them.

I studied bipolar disorder and learned about the medicines I took. I read stories of great characters throughout history, even in current events, who exhibited genius in spite of the highs and lows of mania and depression. I learned how to breathe, how to meditate, how to relax. The St. Elizabeth's team taught me all kinds of techniques to relieve stress and moderate my moods. So many of them are simple things like taking a hot bath, lighting a candle, going for a long walk, or watching a comedy. They also pushed me to spend time with others when I wasn't up for it. All these techniques help tame my moods.

Intellectually, I also understood fitness and nutrition were important components of healthy living, particularly for those with a mental health problem. Admittedly, it would be a long time before I would implement these as part of my lifestyle. I still struggle with sweets and late-night eating, but that's not a mental health issue as much as it is a part of the human condition. I'm fully aware I eat for comfort and pleasure, not because I'm hungry. Though I have to admit, I would be a lot happier if I were thinner while writing for you now.

Fortunately, I've never been much of a drinker. As the years progressed after my diagnosis and my days were spent behind a desk or on sales calls, occasional happy hours at local watering holes would become a welcome part of my life, mainly because I just needed to be around people. For a guy my size, I'm a lightweight; I don't enjoy the drunken feeling as much as I am partial to what it feels like to get high from smoking pot. Again, intellectually, I'm aware of the clinical implications of THC as well as the harm it does to my lungs, and yet, as I've already shared, it seems to do the trick for me and others in friendships and relationships prefer my personality when it's toned down after a hit or two. I smoke alone, privately, almost always by myself. I try as best I can to keep the smell and the paraphernalia out of sight and scent from others. Marijuana is not a social thing for me.

I was lucky to take ownership of my condition from the beginning. I've watched many who deny their mental health problems land in and out of hospitals. If you don't cop to your problems and do something about it, bipolar disorder will own you. Additionally, I believe that not for all, but for most people, if you're diagnosed bipolar, as I was, the concept of getting well and beating the beast, of living a normal, happy, successful life or at least trying to, is a reasonable cognitive choice.

As I was becoming accustomed to the feeling of getting high while at the same time moderated by prescription drugs, the lithium in particular, two books recommended by the Stress Care Center staff were profound game changers for me.

The first, Call Me Anna, is actress Patty Duke's memoir, which describes her years as a child star under the tutelage of her guardians and agents and her descent into major madness. Patty Duke was America's sweetheart of the 1950's, 60's, even into the 70's. At age 13 she starred as Helen Keller in The Miracle Worker on Broadway. Later, she went on to win an Oscar in the film version. She had her own blockbuster hit early sitcom TV show playing dual roles of identical cousins. She won two Golden Globes and three Emmy Awards. Sadly, through it all, she was terribly sick, experiencing delusions and presenting with fits of rage and hostility.

Later in life, she was diagnosed with bipolar disorder. When her doctor explained it to her, she described the moment as being like the flick of a light switch and having a lightbulb go on. It was the same reaction I had experienced with my parents in front of my genial psychiatrist at St Elizabeth's. Patty Duke would become one of the first celebrities to come out of the dark and advocate for the mentally ill, testifying before Congress. She credited Lithium as a lifesaver.

The second book probably had an even greater impact on me. An Unquiet Mind, by Kay Redfield Jamison, who wrote with incredible insight and sensitivity about her experiences as a medical student and young professional. She shares vivid descriptions of her manic episodes expressed in raucous spending sprees and rage. She writes eloquently honestly about deep depression that led to suicide attempts. She comes from the perspective of both the very sick and the healed, having become a revered, renowned international expert on manic depressive disorder and a professor at John Hopkins Medical School, perhaps the best hospital for psychiatry in the United States. An Unquiet Mind has helped millions of people in profound ways and should be considered a must read for those who are bipolar and for their caregivers and loved ones.

A couple of takeaways from these memoirs. First, my illness was not as severe as that of these women. I had maybe short glimpses of clinical psychosis, but often, these ladies were really crazed. When they got their diagnoses, however, each woman came to terms with it. They found their own paths to happy self-actualization in new ways. Their stories helped me realize that there is beauty in the bipolar brain, and that living successfully with it is possible. A second poignancy from these books is that I have found the perspective of bipolar men in literature, on the internet, and in pop culture has been harder to come by, at least any that have resonated for me. While there are famous bipolar actors, journalists, writers, artists, and businessmen in a variety of fields, my guess is that most guys man-up and are reluctant to be vulnerable. The story of Nobel Prize winning mathematician John Nash and his battle with schizophrenia, as portrayed by Russel Crowe in the film A Beautiful Mind, influenced me. Once again, I am lucky never to have experienced his kind of madness. I am grateful that I'm only bipolar. There's rarely a day that goes by when I'm not reminded that someone I know, or someone I love who has some issue or disease far worse than mine. Undoubtedly, in many ways I'm a very lucky man. All in all, I love most of what goes on in my head, the way I experience the human condition, how I feel.

My original episode with Prozac triggered the manic side of my disorder. Prior to that, I only having experienced a few episodes of manic euphoria. Since then, for the most part, serious manic moods manifest themselves should I make the mistake of pulling an all-nighter usually after a rare late night out. For a few days, maybe extending into a week, I experience the need to spend frivolously, no need for sleep, pressured speech, and will start a project or two. Occasionally, my imagination will build up to that keen sense of creativity and invincibility. I can still briefly possess in my own mind the ability to solve great problems. This mood presents once, maybe twice a year. Over the years I've learned to anticipate and even facilitate it. When I find depression tough to shake off, I might allow myself the luxury of a few days of a managed manic high normally expressed in spending. I'm lucky enough to be able to notice what I am doing before I amp up uncontrollably. On the flip side, I'll occasionally allow myself the comfort of a few days of depression. It's a familiar place and sometimes can be a comfort in and of itself. In some ways being depressed feels like my most me. These moods usually follow the pattern surrounding a crash after an anticipated milestone event, almost always after travel.

I've learned that my mood swings occur often, most of the time subtly, sometimes dramatically, throughout the day, every day. I experience frequent, quick cycling ups and downs. I used to confuse this with being an emotional, sympathetic, or empathetic kind of guy. The reality is my brain reacts at any given moment to an array of triggers. Could be a piece of mail, a commercial on TV, or something that happens to me and disrupts that doesn't fit in with my sensibility. My brain takes the bait, and my mood swings quickly up and down as if it could be monitored by a graph like the one tracking the daily ups and downs of the stock market. Medication and lifestyle help to moderate this and keep it manageable. Therapy reminds me not to sweat the small stuff.

As I've shared more than once, most are shocked that to learn I battle mental illness. It's the general sense of joie de vivre that I present publicly which covers the affliction. Those who are the closest to me, however, are frequent witnesses as I experience life's highs and lows. When relationships become close, I make it a point to share my history, so they know to look out for me. A few people on my home team are all given a free pass to check in when they notice I might be trailing off on an extreme.

Within weeks after my release from the St. Elizabeth's Hospital Stress Care Center outpatient program, I was for all intents and purposes reinserted into my life as if nothing had happened. My sister's husband, a vice president of human resources at one of Dayton's largest firms, visited my boss and helped negotiate a return to my job, for a short while on light duty, but within a few months back on track in high pressure sales. I returned to the Rotary Club, the chamber of commerce, and the country club. Knowing that most of my friends and the whole wide sphere of people I knew, almost everyone was aware that I had a breakdown. This was definitely embarrassing and awkward, although there was not much to do but press on, best foot forward and ready with a smile or joke.

I can't say that I went back to work with any zeal. Adjusting to living with medications both at home and on the job was difficult. The side effects from some medications felt the same as depression, including an occasional decent amount of scatter-brained confusion or even occasionally, an all-out high. My psychiatrist agreed that eventually I could at least try to wean myself off some of the drugs. As I worked through this with my docs over the next few years, there were starts and stops on differing prescriptions. Effexor, for example, resulted in bouts of full-on projectile vomiting. After this happened on a sales call, I gave that one up quickly. Depakote gave me flop sweats. I would sit at meetings at the Rotary Club on Friday mornings drenched, the sweat pouring down my reddened face, my hair soaked. A handkerchief my friend in those days.

I was encouraged to participate in a bipolar support group called "Highflyers and Low Landers," which met once a week at Betsy's hospital. This did not last very long, because for me, this group was the pits. Instead of uplifting, the nature of the group was very sad. Their discussions felt like misery loving company to me, really a downer. I couldn't believe that they were talking about shock therapy as an option for their depression.

None of the people in the group worked, all disabled. as far as I could tell, and when I chimed in, I was usually quickly shut down. I gave it up, and spurned support groups for many years.

Work resumed at my chamber of commerce committee. In 1995 the world was shocked when out of the blue, world leaders came to our local Wright Patterson Air Force Base to negotiate the Dayton Peace Accords to end a horrible five years of civil war and ethnic cleansing in Bosnia. My chamber committee focused on commemorations of these events. For the next thirty years I would participate in this process. I met my first head of state in 2000, the first head of the Bosnian triumvirate presidency as negotiated in the Dayton Accords. I introduced him, Dr. Haris Silajdzic, the keynote speaker at our chamber event marking the fifth anniversary of the accords. I enjoyed a small dose of my long given up on a career in diplomacy.

There were definitely numerous stops and starts in my recovery process. A couple of years after my breakdown, I would be fired again by my same boss who, post hospitalization, had given me back my job in the security business. I had not been sick or gone crazy again. I continued to sell very successfully, but the volume of paperwork and administration for the number of leads and clients I generated grew beyond my control. Afterwards, I maintained an uncanny knack for landing on my feet and doing interesting things professionally, although I would be fired from other jobs as time progressed. As always, each job loss felt like a death. Yet another lifetime new low I would have to dig myself out of.

After a while, I refrained from telling Betsy and George when I was between jobs. To protect my parents, I managed my mental health, job losses, and other issues quietly alone. For the rest of their lives, whether I was employed or in very limited financial situations or in any difficulty, as far as my mother and father knew, I was just fine. I managed to live discreetly, quietly, cheaply, occasionally drawing from a modest trust fund from my grandmother and making a generous annual Christmas check from my parents last a long time. Rents from the slum also helped keep me going. I realized years later that Betsy gave us kids just enough extra money to keep us at bay and prevent us from having to go to her when we had problems. George's frequent lament is a constant reminder that as time goes by one's children's problems become fewer, but much, much bigger, and usually much more expensive.

Fairly quickly on the heels of the second firing from my security job, I landed a better position as vice president of sales and marketing with a serious private professional law enforcement company. Our offerings were intense: private corporate security for CEO's; attending high risk firings; strike line security; undercover narcs in schools; and post 9/11 homeland security crisis management planning for schools and corporations.

Our ex-military young high school undercover agents actually lived in rigged apartments in our offices and warehouse. The company conducted early computer forensic training for a local police department which resulted in Dateline's television series "To Catch a Predator." I traveled a decent amount. I consulted on security for nuclear waste that for years had been stockpiled in the basement of the Vanderbilt Clinic in Nashville. I performed security assessments in multiple states. I attended the Governor of Indiana's Summit on Homeland security. I won a federal security bid and traveled to Wellsboro, PA for a contract at the US Geological Surveys Northern Appalachian Research Lab. It was a fascinating situation, and for a couple of years, I made decent money, which coupled with my rents from the slum, made for a pretty good living.

Later, I conducted an assessment at a plant in Cochranton, PA, and got to go by the nearby Allegheny College Campus. Almost twenty years after I had flunked out, it felt strange to spend a couple of hours just walking around. In all those years, never a word from any of my old college buddies. This was three years after my diagnosis; I was still living in "the slum" and doing my thing at Rotary and the country clubs.

Trending towards recovery, I turned 40 in 2003, and it was also a big year for Dayton, OH. As a community we were commemorating the 100th anniversary of the first flight of our local heroes, Orville and Wilbur Wright. I got to participate a bit through my Rotary and Chamber of Commerce memberships. Over the years I had become interested in art, particularly public art, so had gotten to know some excellent local artists through chamber connections. It occurred to me that our sophisticated little hometown of Oakwood could benefit from a public art installation to commemorate Orville and Wilbur's 100th anniversary. Our Rotary committee funded it, and a public art commission ensued. The result was a tall contemporary piece which featured maybe 20 sets of ascending wings in flight strapped on top of tall rods attached to a grid with a large boulder beneath wrapped in chains, signifying that the birds could lift the massive weight together. The wings were mounted on tension rods which could be tuned like a wind chime, but which could also be tightened to mute any noise for neighboring homes. Felt like we did our job after all, beauty being in the eye of the beholder. My friend, the sculptor, shared that during the installation he would arrive at work to find hateful notes from neighbors and passersby complaining about the abstract piece. If we got people motivated to talk about art in our public spaces one way or another, then we were satisfied.

The year 2003 continued to be a standout year for Dayton. President George W. Bush spoke at Wright Patterson Air Force Base, as part of a summer long series of events celebrating the Wright Brothers anniversary called "Inventing Flight." A nearly blighted downtown riverside park became a major national tented exhibition center highlighting manufacturers like Boeing, Lockheed, and McDonnell

Douglas. For a few brief shining weeks, this drew a lot of attention to our community. The Dayton Dragons' semi-pro baseball team were in their third hit season in a brand-new downtown riverfront stadium. Adjacent to the stadium, there was a cool new Five Rivers Fountain which had been installed on the Great Miami River. Five plumes that shoot 200 feet high and 400 feet across are lit by towers which create a laser show in the mist. All of this held in conjunction with a majorly amped up annual United States Air Force Air Show held at Dayton Airport, which every year is one of the most exciting and top airshows in the world. At this point, things seemed to be looking up for our town, and for me, and I was excited to be a part of it.

At about the same time, I was conducting a security assessment at a plant in a neighborhood that bordered Oakwood. It was on a street which had featured a favorite local bakery and convenience store in a colonial-looking building that had a local landmark architecturally perfect copper cupola with a weathervane on top of it. My client had bought the old bakery and tore it down to make space for the new building that I was assessing for access control and surveillance cameras. As we made our tour, I noticed the old cupola in weeds set out in a field. "What are you going to do with that?" I asked my customer. Eventually, again through Rotary, money was raised, and a nice big gazebo topped by the old historic copper cupola was built on the grounds of the nearby Patterson Homestead, the original home of John Patterson who invented the cash register. The homestead sits on the edge of Oakwood and the University of Dayton campus. The new gazebo is a peaceful spot in the neighborhood as well as part of Homestead's offerings as a wedding venue.

Then another ugly end to a job. Once again it felt like the end of the world to me. The owner of our private law enforcement group passed away, and things went sour with the business. My big federal contract at the Northern Appalachian Research Lab was going south at the time, my position was tenuous already. Although it was getting much harder to remain optimistic, I stayed the course hoping that I would land successfully on my feet again. As usual, I left Betsy and George in the dark. Although, by this time I was convinced that my mother especially was turning a self-protective blind eye to my problems. I expect she knew when I was in trouble. She did not miss much. After a while, I did score another job, but as one would expect, the older I got, the longer it would take for the next opportunity to present itself and come to fruition. Both my age and track record were becoming obstacles impacting on the quality and profitability of any work I might find.

Never really feeling stigmatized or marginalized, It was during these years that I started to share my journey of mental illness with others. Many people knew I was willing to talk and share my experiences with anyone who might be in trouble. I received one of these out of the blue calls from a gal I had known since 5th grade. Kathy and I had sung together all the way through high school, even acting together in "South Pacific" our senior year. She'd played Bloody Mary. She was in the middle of an ugly divorce from one of the guys who was on the Oakwood football team that I had helped coach who was also a member of the Oakwood Rotary with me. "Would you go check on Paul?" she asked. "I think he might be suicidal." I drove over to his new house, running into his brother-in-law who had arrived to get his guns, rifles, and ammunition out of the place. When I arrived, Paul was painting a new bedroom for their three-year-old twin sons. There was nothing going on there that gave me any concern, so I reported to Kathy everything seemed OK. While I hadn't known Paul well, our paths had crossed occasionally, and we actually really hit it off well on this awkward occasion. This turned into an unexpected transformational friendship and partnership.

Paul and his associates were in commercial real estate and were in the process of a major business acquisition in Downtown Dayton which included 11 commercial buildings, one an entire block of dilapidated historic structures, and the pearl: a parking management company that owned or managed 20,000 parking spaces downtown, at the Dayton Airport, and at local hospitals. It was a big endeavor for a small team. I was hired as a consultant to help manage all of this. I had found my next interesting career reinvention.

CHAPTER 10

BAVARIA AND BOSNIA

To my great frustration, I worked unpaid by Paul for several months, reminiscent of my early unpaid days in the nation's Capital. As this drew on, a buddy from my chamber experience who was on the Dayton City Council, suggested I join Dayton's delegation for an upcoming official visit to Sarajevo and Augsburg, Germany, Dayton's sister cities. It was the kind of thing I would normally turn down. This would be the first time I experienced what would later become a mantra for me. That is to just say "YES!" I could attend with Dayton's Mayor, council members, a museum director, a local news anchor, and officials from the University of Dayton. "Why me?" I wondered. I was a practically unemployed college dropout. Certainly, known as bipolar by many already. Why would I represent our town in this way? I was 41, and other than a drunken night at Niagara Falls with fraternity brothers at Allegheny, I had never left the country. I didn't even have a passport.

I had been experiencing a smoldering depression on the heels of my last job termination and money was becoming tight waiting for a paycheck as this new position developed. Still, I had a passport expedited and within a few weeks was off to Germany. The excitement of the trip sucked the depression out of me quickly, and I escalated into a pretty good, but level manic high over the course of the journey.

After a long flight to Munich and a couple of hours by train, nine of us arrived at our hotel in Bavaria. We were jet-lagged & exhausted, but that same afternoon, we headed to Oktoberfest in Germany! I couldn't believe it. Finally, if only for a little while, I felt like I was experiencing the life I had expected! For three days, the town of Augsburg rolled out the red carpet for us.

Our day of overseas travel and drinking from big steins overflowing with strong German beer was followed that same first evening by a dinner in our honor at Augsburg City Hall. Still on the move since we woke up in Ohio, we pulled ourselves together quickly back in our hotel and dressed up in our dark suits and ties. We boarded the lux touring full size coach bus the town had chartered for us for our visit and were delivered to their beautiful municipal building. Up four flights on a grand marble staircase to the top floor we marched. As imposing doors were opened for us, the unexpected sight of the Augsburg Golden Hall knocked our socks off. Blinding gold everywhere, there were even gilded murals on the ceiling. We found ourselves by surprise in one of the most significant Renaissance-style rooms of its type in Europe.

As we entered, a string quartet began playing Mozart as a fanfare. Servers in starched uniforms were waiting with flutes of champagne on silver platters. Augsburg's mayor wore the gold collar of his office around his neck and was flanked by an official greeting party. All of us perhaps still slightly buzzed and exhausted Midwesterners turned to look at the elaborate doors through which we had just entered to see who was coming in behind us. Who was this group in front of us making all the fuss about? We couldn't believe that all of this was just for us. As for me, finally being in Europe was over the top, but to be treated like a dignitary in a gilded hall in the process was on another level. This was like something out of a movie. Fortunately, my pre-travel mood swing from slight depression to a mild manic good mood had put me in a pretty good place to experience this and engage.

Following a cocktail reception, we were removed to a smaller adjacent room for dinner, maybe thirty guests in total. This room was the exact same design as the Golden Hall, except there was no gilding, instead it was all highly varnished carved wood, really spectacular. The only other individual at my table who spoke English was an older Egyptian man, a new kind of diverse experience for me.

The next day we recuperated and managed some sightseeing, including the obligatory Bavarian brewery tour. That evening, we returned to the Golden Hall as guests at a municipal function during which a local German philanthropist was presented with the key to the city. This was a big event, with perhaps 300 in attendance, all dressed to the nines. In comparison, they must have thought us dowdy Ohio folk had come right out of the 1950's. Following another champagne reception, our Dayton delegation was escorted to front row seats and given headphones for our translator. There were long speeches, followed by several performances, including as a finale a group of boys and young men who were dressed and sounded just like the Vienna Boys Choir. This was a big deal. Unfortunately, as the speeches wore on and the room got warmer, most everyone in our travel weary group in the front row very noticeably nodded our heads as we dozed off, the German to English translation in our ears lulling us to sleep. Not a great showing for us.

After another day of sightseeing in Germany, we returned to Munich for a flight to Bosnia. Immediately upon arrival, the difference between our two sister cities was strikingly apparent. As we drove from the Sarajevo airport to downtown, we passed one depressing, tall cement hi-rise apartment building after another. They loomed over the spires of ages old minarets like a blanket of communism. Although the landscape and culture in the Balkans differed in so many ways from our German experience, the people we met in both communities were the same. All kind, and very welcoming. They were all engaged, eager to impress and show us the best hospitality they possibly could. We were overwhelmed by it in both cities.

In Germany, our ride had been that very sleek, squeaky clean, and beautifully engineered motor coach complete with a dining area and galley. In Bosnia we traveled in a caravan of six or seven dark Volkswagen Passat sedans followed by a couple of minivans. It took me a few days in the former Olympic City of Sarajevo before I realized that the men in dark suits who were lurking in front of our hotel or milling around smoking as we arrived at venues were actually our security detail. We were also followed by a small cadre of Bosnian reporters, photographers, and sometimes a television crew. As a result, we would watch ourselves on televisions back at our hotel as we appeared on the local evening news, a surreal experience. None of us were fluent in Serbo-Croat, so we wondered what they were reporting about us.

We stayed at an easily recognizable Holiday Inn that had been built for the 1984 Olympics. The effects of decades of communist dictatorship was palpable. Evidence of five years of brutal warfare and mass ethnic genocide was everywhere, most prominently in the freshly painted white crosses marking graves. In almost any greenspace, everywhere you looked, along highways and on boulevards, on street corners, bordering parks, and on mountain passes a sea of crosses were crowded all nestled under a skyline of minarets from the mosques. So sadly stunning.

Nine years had passed since the ceasefire had been negotiated in Dayton. Our Peace Accords and its temporary measures were installed and were on the way to becoming institutionalized. To describe the politics of Bosnia, Serbia, and Croatia, and the history that brought them to this point is way beyond my capabilities. That's for statesmen and genius intellects, not me. I can, however, accurately characterize the Bosnian people I met as beleaguered, exhausted, and forever scarred. Yet, they were also incredibly motivated, hardworking, and hopeful, regardless of what they had been through. They witnessed grandmothers scrambling to hide behind overturned buses to dodge snipers as they went about their daily business, looking for hard-to-come-by food and supplies. Bullet holes and bomb pockmarks create a mosaic all over buildings throughout the city like graffiti, and yet the Bosnian people I have come to know all seem to focus intently on the future.

Our goodwill trip went far beyond a typical sister cities exchange. There was a breakfast meeting at the Holiday Inn with the US Ambassador, followed a couple of days later by a second meeting with the Ambassador at the American Embassy, our little caravan subject to screenings for bombs and explosive devices. Our mayor met with at least one of the three sitting rotating Bosnian presidents. We dedicated trees, toured galleries, museums, the usual. All of us made remarks at a televised council meeting at Sarajevo City Hall. Sitting at a foreign municipal conference room table, American flags, and our names on placards in front of each of our places, headphones on for our translators, responding to questions from reporters was interesting for a guy on his first overseas adventure for sure.

We didn't have to look hard beyond the scars of war to find beauty in Bosnian culture. Their traditional kebab, rather like Bob Evans sausage links on steroids, were served at almost every meal along with Slivovica, the strong plum brandy that will knock most Americans out after a single shot. It's so strong that it can kill almost anything that ails you. Sarajevo's ancient open-air market, the Bascarsija, is an ancient wonder. One small shop after another in buildings and stalls so old they look like caves. The color and aroma of the fruits and vegetables, seafood, bread, and spices are all intoxicating. There are textiles, jewelry, and elaborate sets for brewing and serving Turkish Coffee, most of it displayed spilling out of crates. I had never experienced anything like it. We hung out here every day during our visit. The mountainous landscape that surrounded the city was flush and verdant and peppered with colorful red tile roofs. This was the first time I had visited a city where the Adhan was recited on loudspeakers for the call to prayer, which five times a day reminded us we were very far away from home.

We toured the Sarajevo Tunnel which had been dug by hand from the basement of a house at the end of the airport tarmac. During the war, people and intelligence alike were smuggled in and out of the city in this underground tunnel of hope. The abandoned Olympic ski jump venue was a sad sight to see, crumbling in a field of feral cats. We dined at a restaurant that overlooked the Miljacka River and the ancient Latin Bridge, which was built during the Ottoman Empire, historic for its proximity to the site of the assassination of Archduke Ferdinand in 1915. We had lunch at a new hillside nine-hole layout on the outskirts overlooking the city. I was told that at the time this was the only golf course in Bosnia.

I was proud of our hometown on this tour. In Bosnia, our Ohio delegation was supplemented by a group of musicians from the Dayton Philharmonic Orchestra and student musicians from Dayton's new high school for the performing arts. A young Maestro, Dino Zonic, who had fled Bosnia to Dayton during the war returned home with us to premiere a piece he had composed to honor his country. Together with the professionals from our philharmonic, Ohio high schoolers filled the remaining empty seats in the war-compromised Sarajevo Philharmonic Orchestra. The blended group of musicians played beautifully. My understanding was that this was the first full symphony orchestra performance in Sarajevo's National Theatre since the war had broken out. It was very moving, and strange to be asked to stand and be recognized as a VIP guest in a full house in a historic auditorium in a foreign country.

Twice in Bosnia, I broke out my Michael Jackson moves. The first time was at a dinner where a small combo played Bosnian folk music. Word got around that I could dance and can't help myself when anything from Thriller is playing, so the bass player started to pluck the first bars of Billie Jean, and I was egged on, not entirely reluctant. Admittedly, Michael Jackson's moves performed on my huge frame are unexpected and hilarious. The second time was at our final goodbye dinner, which was held in the Olympic figure skating venue where Katarina Witt and Scott Hamilton had won their gold medals twenty years prior in 1984. Here everyone danced to more tunes from Michael Jackson followed by more folk dancing and lots of hugs. We flew back to Munich for an overnight layover before heading home to Ohio.

Our group congregated at Munich's New Town Hall just in time to witness the Rauthaus Glockenspiel Clock Tower and its famous bears and other characters spin around it. At this point, our Mayor had had enough of our group, and suddenly headed off on her own. Instinctively, I took her arm, and the two of us set off on our own personal German shopping excursion. This would be the beginning of an unexpected great friendship for both of us.

Rhine McLin served in the Ohio State Senate, had two terms as Mayor of Dayton, and later briefly served as Chair of the Ohio Democratic Party. She held the position of vice chair as well, and is a major get out the vote advocate today. Life for those of us who grew up in Oakwood could not have been more different than her background growing up in the black community on Dayton's west side. The two areas were on opposite sides of the Miami River, and literally on opposite sides of railroad tracks. On our flight on the trip from Dayton to Munich, Rhine and I, who had never met, were assigned seats next to each other. For four hours, I slept next to her soon to be diagnosed with sleep apnea. I snored and snorted, bobbed, and drooled, and rolled my head on and off her shoulder all the way to Germany while she did crossword puzzles. With that auspicious start we have enjoyed a great friendship. Just a life tip arising from my friendship with Rhine. Take wonder in every individual you come across in any situation whether it be in business, social circumstances, or in line at the grocery store. Look beyond your own borders and across any cultural divide and get to know as many folks as you can with different perspectives. It's one of the healthiest and most rewarding things a person can do to improve their own lives.

After our return from this trip, my credibility increased with my new boss Paul and his business partners. Accordingly, I was assigned a leadership role in the parking business, and happily started receiving decent paychecks. I took over management of 115 of their employees, as well as 40 more in a hospital valet parking operation. Our contracts, including several with the City of Dayton were big ones. Paul and his partners left it up to me to present monthly billing reports to several of the company's largest clients. Sitting across from executives in some of our town's most important boardrooms, I had to be the guy to explain away excess management fees for paving, parking space striping, power washing, snow plowing, in short, all those line items from which the partners earned additional perhaps unanticipated revenue. I was good at appeasing clients whose anticipated revenue was often impacted.

I drank more during this job than any other time in my career. There were happy hours, lots of them. There were also boozy weekends spent by the pool Paul had built for his bachelor pad. As their dad's good friend, his three-year old twins became my little buddies. Paul successfully talked me out of the Oakwood lifestyle he had just left when he divorced. In due course, I quit both Rotary and country clubs. In short order Paul agreed to buy the slum from me. I moved into one of the slightly swanky apartments on the nearby Kettering, Ohio, civic grounds, a complex that many folks we knew used as a decent place to live while transitioning through a divorce. I could hear summer concerts from the adjacent outdoor performing arts pavilion which every year had an excellent concert season. I really enjoyed pre-concert daytime rehearsals and soundchecks at home alone on my balcony from the likes of Chicago, Earth Wind & Fire, Cheryl Crowe, and Willie Nelson.

Leaving the slum and creating a new environment and a simpler lifestyle and focusing on my mental health-unencumbered was good for me. I was definitely healing, so much so that I was able to have relationships. Just a few years later, when I finally crossed the Ohio River Bridge headed south for the last time, I left behind two women. The second being a broken engagement with a beautiful Ukrainian woman. I was also a dad in training for both of these women. Daughters age 3, 5, & 8, with the first, a blond divorcee from our Dayton circle. My Ukrainian's fiancée's daughter was maybe age 10 when we met and barely off the boat from Kiev with extremely broken rudimentary English. Both of these relationships were so much fun, with great times and lots of laughs. Even our break-ups went OK. I still stay in touch with them through social media. These women are still connections in the thread of my life as it goes forward.

However, as tradition would have it, after maybe two and a half years with the company, I was betrayed and fired by Paul as part of the fallout when the big real estate deal and parking management company we were all involved in became too complicated. My professional opportunities compromised more than ever; I was forced to take a position once again in the yellow pages industry. Just two years later, I was fired again as a yellow page account executive. As always, into mourning for two consecutive job losses I would go, with few options left in what was becoming a tarnished professional reputation.

With minimal options and a legacy of unfulfilled promise, I figured it was time for me to get the hell out of Ohio. It had become time to reinvent in a new dynamic. I had squirreled away enough money to keep me afloat for two or three years before I would run out of cash. I kept my latest failures off George and Betsy's radar screen. As usual, If they asked about my work and how things were going, I would lie and say, "Everything is great!" I could have been out of work six or eight months before I might announce a new job as if I had just resigned from the old one for something better.

CHAPTER 11

AT THE BEACH

It was 2009, and I was 45 years old. I lied and told my parents that I had found a new job and would move to Hilton Head where my grandparents had settled forty years earlier. By this time, Betsy and George had also bought a home there as well and were dividing their time between Dayton and Hilton Head. My grandmother Connie had maintained her home there in large part because she thought Betsy and George would inherit it and move in. Instead, our grandparents' house was left intact as if she had just left for errands for twenty years after she died, and available for vacationing grandchildren. This would be my escape hatch.

So, when Betsy and George made their move back to Ohio for the summer and fall, I pulled the reverse, making my own permanent move to Hilton Head. Crossing the Ohio River bridge into Kentucky was a huge milestone, and a profoundly emotional one. Yet, by the time I reached Hilton Head eleven hours later, I had already turned a page on a new chapter. Although I was once again unemployed and all of my triggers for depression were firing, this move signaled my entry into long-term recovery.

That knack I have for landing on my feet served me well. I was allowed to move into my grandparents' fabulous home in the prestigious Sea Pines Resort temporarily while I settled in a new beach town, started a new career, and found my own home. By the time I arrived at my grandparents' place to make it my escape hatch from Ohio, Betsy and George had been snowbirds for a decade, their spot just a short bike ride away. My siblings, cousins, and I, just the five of us, would use our long-deceased grandma's house for vacations for as few as three weeks a year in total. Other than my grandparents' wardrobes, sterling silver, and some of the best fine art, the house was completely intact, left almost as if the clock had stopped when grandma died. Everything remained immaculate. It was an obviously high-class time warp in a world-class location, and a great landing pad for me as I figured out my next steps. My level of living in my latest down and out and unemployed circumstances was quite an improvement on Hilton Head where I was surrounded by the best that money could buy. Not bad for an unemployed guy.

I tried a couple of jobs that had been advertised on Craigslist, but neither panned out. Instead, with money in the bank and time on my hands, I enrolled at the University of South Carolina Beaufort's new Hilton Head Gateway Campus just off the island on the mainland. The University had a new adult degree program for nontraditional students (usually meaning old people), and I took advantage of it.

For a year and a half, on Wednesdays and Saturdays, with some extra online classes, I was once again a full-time college student. This was my fourth attempt at yet another excellent institution of higher learning to complete my college degree. Ten years later, I have yet to walk to the stirring strains of "Pomp and Circumstance" other than at my high school graduation. One more major life goal still out there left to achieve. I suppose essentially my education is my largest ever started, but never finished project.

Only one of the classes I took at USCB has continued to resonate. It was called "Coastal Environment of the Southeastern United States." Our slightly hippish adjunct lady professor was terrific. The class and its lab work concentrated on our local Lowcountry ecosystem.

I learned a tremendous amount about the amazing environment that my grandparents and the rest of us fell in love with in 1969. I learned what it means to live on a "beach ridge variegated barrier island." Our flora, fauna, and all that surrounds us here on Hilton Head leave even the most stoic individuals breathless. It is a strikingly beautiful, even awe-inspiring landscape. Our beaches and tidal salt marsh estuaries abound with schools of rare strand-feeding bottlenose dolphins. Almost everywhere you turn, there is something rare and beautiful in nature that can make your eyes pop wide open and will provide peace to the soul if you let it. I know this is true. Three million visitors come here every year, year after year, confirm it. I am beyond confident that this gorgeous place just in and of itself has been a key component in my improved mental health.

Hilton Head is an amalgam of native people and transplants, and it continues to evolve. Most of us are from somewhere else. The great majority of residents and visitors hail from the Buckeye State like us. Charles Fraser, the genius who developed Hilton Head's Sea Pines Plantation in the '60's and '70's, spent nearly all of his marketing budget in Ohio, Columbus, Cleveland, Cincinnati, and Dayton. His team figured Ohio's awful winters, coupled with only a one day's drive time, made it the perfect place to target market their new resort. It worked like magic. We came in droves from Ohio to HHI.

Given my family's history here, there were plenty of opportunities for me to fit in quickly, although just about everyone I knew on the island were friends of my parents and grandparents. The average age of my acquaintances on the island ranged between 70-90 years old. These were wonderful longtime good friends, but not a great crowd for a reinventing guy hoping for a semblance of a social life in a new town. Fortunately, right off the bat after my arrival, I connected with childhood Oakwood friends, two sisters whose middle brother was in my class, on our football team, and part of my clan of good buddies in both elementary school and high school. By coincidence, they lived together literally a block and two fairways away from my Grandparents' home where I was enjoying rent-free safe harbor. They took me in immediately like a brother and have been like close family to me here ever since.

It was not long before I moved out of my grandparents' crib. These sisters hooked me up with a friend who had a sleek furnished one-bedroom condo just off HHI's popular Shelter Cove Harbor with a dazzling 180-degree deep water view across beautiful Broad Creek, which cuts across the middle of the island. The complex of two five story buildings was gated with a fantastic waterfront pool and hot tub. My apartment was spacious, bright, and desirable. Yachts, sailboats, speedboats, and kayakers went by constantly. It was an impressive view and was by far the coolest place I had ever lived in my adult life. The neighborhood was so hopping that every Tuesday night during the summer tourist season, fireworks are shot off from a barge. This good was living for a 45-year-old unemployed full-time student.

At just about the same time I moved into that condo, I landed a job in advertising sales with the local newspaper "The Island Packet." I was ready to get back into the career field, and eager to stop lying to George and Betsy about my job prospects. It had been one and a half years since I had last earned any income, and I was excited about it, although my start with the company was auspicious, but not in a good way.

As always in a new sales position, my initial results were very, very good. Right out of the gate, armed with my fantastic Yellow Pages sales training, I was bringing in big contracts, impressing my new bosses. As usual, I was a happy, get along with others on the team kind of employee. I was quickly a great addition to their sales team. I felt validated immediately. Then, within weeks, in a hurry to get to the office, I totaled my car and two others in a bad crash literally right in front of the Island Packet office.

Except for a concussion, I was for the most part uninjured. Two weeks later, however, I was called into the HR office with the results of my Worker's Comp urinalysis. "Um, uh, you tested positive for marijuana on your urine test, Bob," explained the nice HR director. "No doubt." I replied. But I couldn't believe it, they kept me on board. As long as I passed urinalysis drug testing three months in a row, I could keep my job. This was a huge break, and I managed to do it.

The day after the accident was an odd afternoon, as I had an ice pack strapped to my head for the concussion, but still went to the beach with friends who were nice enough to get me out. While we were sunbathing and tipping a few cold beverages, probably not too smart right after the accident. Anyway, I was introduced to a woman who ran some sort of international business which involved students. I didn't really get the gist of the business, but I told her that I had always wanted to travel and would be interested if she had any openings in the future.

With the drug screening episode behind me, the job at the newspaper quickly became boring. The curse of bipolarity that limited career choices often led to professional prospects wherein the work was below my capabilities. Boredom and a sense of daily monotony set in. After almost twenty-five years of hardcore, pavement pounding sales jobs, I was getting burnt out. Besides, because I'd been gaining a lot of weight, an obese salesman is often considered sloppy by buyers and employers. I did not realize it until afterwards, but clearly, my personal appearance was having an impact on my client's buying decisions.

CHAPTER 12

MOOD SWINGS ON A GLOBAL LEVEL

I reached out after a year to the world traveling businesswoman, I had met on the beach with an icepack on my head asking her if she was ready to really market her business. The answer was yes! Back at the newspaper, this resulted in one of the very few times that I had ever quit a sales position instead of being fired from it. I will always be grateful to the cool management team at the newspaper who kept me on after my workman's comp pot blip. My new employer was aware of this habit up front. I was brought on board as vice president of sales and marketing and had once again rebounded professionally into an interesting situation.

To sum up, the nature of this business isn't easy. Most resort communities like Hilton Head simply do not have a sufficiently large enough local employee base to serve the huge influx of tourists that drive the economy. Employers turn to companies like ours to recruit seasonal international talent to fill hundreds of positions in culinary, food and beverage, housekeeping, activities, and loss prevention. Our company, like others across the country, was designated by the Department of State to recruit and provide temporary work visas to foreign university students earning hospitality degrees overseas who needed internships to complete their programs.

Suddenly, I was on the absolute lowest ring of any position in Hillary Clinton's, then John Kerry's Department of State as an "alternate responsible officer" for the J-1 Visa program. A hilarious aside for me, as I was once again a lifelong Republican doing his thing in another Democrat administration. Had this job come around years ago following my experience in Washington on Capitol Hill in the 1980's, it would have been a decent next step in a diplomatic career. Instead, pushing age 50, it was the best beach job I could ever have hoped for.

While we served almost all of Hilton Head's major resorts and attractions, the company's clientele extended far beyond. We provided international interns to some of the most famous hotels and resorts in the United States, including Memphis's Peabody, The Broadmoor Hotel and Little Nell in Colorado, San Ysidro Ranch and the Ritz Carlton in Santa Barbara, and the Fontainebleau and Setai Hotels in Miami Beach, to name a few. Our 500-property database was a who's who of the best hotels nationwide. The list of glamorous places we served across the country was like a menu for the landed rich. What unbelievable experiences these unknowing foreign students would have, working and learning at these luxurious places.

After a few months of training, I was off on my first overseas recruiting trip. At each stop we made; we would hold job fairs usually in European hotel ballrooms attended by anywhere from as few as 30 to as many as 300 potential hires. In their interviews, all of these young international students would tell us in broken English that their lifetime dream was to come to America. Our hosts when traveling were our overseas cooperating agencies who had ties with foreign universities to promote the program. They were monitored both by the State Department and by us to comply with stringent immigration regulations. As such, we were treated like dignitaries on these junkets. After all, we were officially designated by the State Department as public diplomats, and we were offering temporary jobs and trips of a lifetime for young students to great places in the USA.

My role on these trips was as primary presenter, the front man. I would first cover the program's rules and regulations, then give presentations about the potential employers for which the students were interviewing. Often these were formal functions. In Asia, for example, the events would include playing of national anthems, speeches, the whole bit. Once the students' visas were approved, my job evolved to become their primary contact and uncle/mentor while they were in the United States. The travel, work, and internships were not easy for all of them. I provided moral support and occupational direction to the kids. At any one given time, we shared responsibility for in the range of 1000 foreign students and managed housing on Hilton Head as manager for 300 hundred more overseas foreign adult workers who come back and forth every year from mainly the Caribbean to earn their living. They are crucial to keeping the wheels of the hospitality industry turning on this island. With my janky last name too hard to pronounce for most of them, I was given the international moniker of "Mr. Bob." I would soon become known as this alter ego in a surprising number of countries around the globe.

We were treated exceptionally well in every city. We visited the best restaurants, had gift exchanges, toured cultural heritage sites, and at almost every stop were given national folk dancing demonstrations. Usually about a third of our visits were business-related, with the remainder being small group cultural exchanges. We would generally visit three or four countries on each seven-to-ten-day trip, and generally enjoyed deluxe accommodations, food, and liquor. With the exception of flights, almost all of it comped by our overseas cooperators.

These trips to places like Istanbul, Sophia, Bulgaria, Kyiv, Skopje Macedonia, Belgrade, Pristina, Kosovo, and later to the Philippines and Thailand were personally and professionally gratifying, although not without my occasional bipolar foibles. For example, my pants fell down to my ankles while televised in front of a crowded ballroom of people in Macedonia. It happened again in the Istanbul airport, but that was because I had to take off my belt at security. On another occasion, with a traveling associate, we broke into helpless church giggles and eventually, barrel laughs at a tour guide in Belgrade who went on so long and boringly with local history, we just could not take it. Once I very awkwardly broke down in tears at a business dinner in Manila and had to leave the table, only to return and do it all over again. This time, the reason was valid. My mother Betsy had just been diagnosed with stage IV lung cancer, and I felt so terrible for her and all of us, and helpless at a distance of 10,000 miles, thus my ugly crying at a business dinner in the Philippines.

The other integral part of my job was business development when we were not traveling overseas. In that role, I was in charge of monitoring existing and bringing on new host employees. This provided the opportunity to visit luxury properties to help employers manage their programs and comply with State Department regulations. I brought the historic King and Prince Beach and Golf Resort and the Cloister at Sea Island on board. Nearly 200 students from all over the world descended for two seasons on St. Simons Island, Ga.

Trips to the glamorous Cloister had long been a family tradition for senior members of our family, back when it was a bit more affordable and before the historic buildings had been torn down and replaced with a more modern resort. Connie and Bob would vacation there from time to time. Later, as a widow, Grandma would take Betsy, Nancy, and their husbands there for a couple of days to celebrate birthdays. We kids even got to go once, and it was spectacular. Everyone but I got early check-ins, availability of my room delayed as Margaret Thatcher's party had been late on their departure. Indeed, this place and its guests are in a league of their own. For two years as a major vendor, I was occasionally given a complimentary $1,300 a night suite accommodation. I was not unaware that, in a roundabout way, I was finally living the lifestyle and enjoying the favorite places of the people I loved and respected the most. I did not mind if, compared to my predecessors, I was going through the service entrance to be a part of it. The experience of it was close enough to the real thing for me.

As for my mood, I had been weaning off any bipolar medication for probably five years or more. I would see a psychiatrist once a year at this point, sit for a therapy session, and ask, "So, do you think I'm sane Doc?" The response was always the same. My physicians would compliment me for having a savvy sense of self and an excellent understanding of my own mental health issues and how to handle them. I had not really experienced any major depression or manic phases that I couldn't manage with the skills that I had learned at the Stress Care Center 10 years prior. There might be an occasional depression I found tough to shake, usually around a life pattern I could predict often after a milestone or travel, When this happened, I would get a prescription for Prozac or one of the other boutique replacements for it. I would only need to take them just a few weeks to purge the bad mood. I had only used this technique maybe two or three times in the past five years.

As savvy as I had become about my moods, however, something else was happening with my brain chemistry during these years. I was again clueless, just as my parents and I had been in the years before my bipolar diagnosis. Long story short, I had become enormous. My weight had ballooned for the second time to more than three hundred pounds. Over the next few years, I would gain another fifty. I am already a big-boned guy, but I had expanded to ogre-like proportions.

I didn't see it. Instead, when I looked at myself in the mirror, I saw a handsome, somewhat husky guy in slimming clothes. The reality of it was that my head had literally grown in size, my cheeks, face and neck, even my shoulders all looked as if they had been overinflated from the inside. I carry the weight from the waist up and I was growing a big expanding barrel chest and pot belly. With a booming voice and the energy I put out, my overall presence was even bigger than it was reflected on the scale, upon which I rarely stood. I would ignore this for years, never making a connection between my mood and binge eating.

There were other symptoms of my bipolar disorder. I still had trouble keeping my vehicle and personal space efficiently clean. Although I finally had a place that merited guests, it required a herculean day of cleaning and dealing with piles of dirty clothes before anyone could arrive. When the doorbell rang, I was usually still sweating from the effort to pull the place together, and friends were greeted by the essence of a heavy-handed trigger of various cleaning supplies. I had gotten way better about this than I had been in the past when my environments were closing in on hoarding. I worked hard on it finally, devoting every Saturday morning to keeping house, but I could never quite get the whole relatively small space immaculate. Still the environment and the outstanding view, the sunsets, and the fact that friends could pick me up in their boats from a dock at home was unbelievable.

Here comes another direct tip to bipolar patients, their friends, family, and caregivers. George always said to us growing up, that the environment is important. It was not until I had a place of my own that I could be proud of that I realized how right my father was. The condition of my living quarters over the years was both evidence of and triggers for depression. I have found that once a bad environment is institutionalized in a household, it's hard to bring it back. Living alone and never having friends or family in your home is unhealthy. Having people in your home allows friendships and relationships to go to the next level. If you're single and embarrassed to bring dates into your home, building any future with someone in this way is difficult. Isolation is a social red flag.

Aside from weight gain and housekeeping, other triggers of my beautiful but bipolar mind were taxes, bills, and dental work. I had always had an irrational fear and stress paralysis when it came to bureaucracies of any kind, including the DMV, insurance co-payments, and the like. Crucial paperwork that came in the mail would get stashed in drawers, unanswered for a lot of my adult life. Simple things like keeping the car registration up to date and maintaining my car insurance cards in the glove compartment never seemed within my reach. I just could not keep these simple details together. I had no debt or any financial problems; my bills and living expenses were always minimal and manageable. I had, however, established a bad credit rating. I was like a drinker in denial about this. Like the old joke, "I drink, I get drunk, I fall down, no problem." I did not experience my financial problems simply because I ignored them.

This went on for a generation. For a few years, I was even in failure to file status with tax agencies at all levels, especially the IRS. I was living in fear. At least once a week, I'd think to myself, "I've got to figure out how to do my taxes." This was both sad and scary, as I had always prided myself on good citizenship. Finally, I had the resources and good sense to hire a good Hilton Head tax attorney. To my surprise and relief, the upshot of all my late filings was perfect compliance with all of my taxes and a five-figure windfall of tax refunds I had never filed to receive. I'm now a raging stickler on all things like this, having come to my own conclusion about something George used to preach which is that often-taking action when it is hard to do eliminates much bigger stressors down the line.

Yet another lesson for bipolar patients or those on their care teams when it comes to situations like my aforementioned civic and financial issues: never be afraid to ask for help. Let's face it, everyone, from the healthiest person to those with mood disorders, will fall into bad habits from time to time, or find themselves feeling at the edge of a cliff. Unfortunately, most of us are raised to project the notion that we can manage our own affairs, thank you very much, and that asking for help is embarrassing or even bad manners. A fall into old and lazy habits and bad patterns can be more devastating to those with mood disorders than it is for others, resulting in relapse into psychosis or other behaviors that trigger deeper problems. Never hesitate to ask for help whether you have a support system or not. If you can, find a way to get help when you need it, regardless of the source. Do not be shy or proud about it. Ask for help, and then follow through on it. It's likely that you will be happy with the result. Then be on the lookout for someone who might benefit from your help. Bipolar individuals often tend to be hyper-focused on their maladies and their own personal agenda to the point where they are unable to be empathetic to the needs of others, often intentionally landing themselves in the self-fulfilling role of family martyr. A clear noticeable difference I experienced when good mental health became a consistent part of my life, was the joy and gratification that came when I focused on others rather than self.

Caregivers should be aware that the more we push loved ones and friends away, the more likely it is that we are in trouble. Most of us perform with such obvious patterns our impending breakdowns are almost always chock full of warnings. Unfortunately, often emotionally exhausted, hopeful loved ones turn a self-protective blind eye to these obvious clues. Then they are shocked to discover their loved one is living in squalor, is taking dangerous long drives and middle of the night manic shopping runs, or worse, loved ones who have lulled themselves into a naïve sense that everything is going to be ok, are shocked to receive a call about their son, daughter, or spouse from a jail or hospital. It's likely, in any bipolar career, that we are far sicker than we will ever let on to you. Most bipolar patients are in denial, and most of us are very defensive, often to the point of drawing deep lines in the sand. Defensive walls will surround us when triggers and hot buttons are pressed. Persevere as long as you can. Do not be afraid to cross boundary lines to help get better life results. This may end in resentment, but when and if you can get through, remain hopeful they will ultimately appreciate it. Go at it with the best you can love and without judgment.

A common thread for many caregivers might feel like failure. You may never be able to crack the surface of the bipolar brain and help your loved one. In a sad percentage of cases, parents and loved ones may not be able to help the new stranger in their lives. The patient might blame or even shame projecting their life disappointments on to you. The emotional baggage of loving a mentally ill individual is often so great that many caregivers have to take a pass for their own salvation. Being bipolar sucks the life not only out of those of us who live with it, but also draws blood from the ones who love and try to care for us in a different way. Should you find yourself among those who are unable to help their own loved ones, my advice is to manage your own self-care first. Maybe you know another family member, friend, pastor, neighbor, or organization who is the right shoulder and resource for your loved one. There exists a whole world of wonderful mental health advocacy on a level never before seen which far too many people fail to take advantage of. To be honest, nowadays just mention in a group setting that someone in your family is struggling with depression, and no doubt someone in the room will chime in to share. It is not a bad idea to get to know these folks who go through the same pain you experience. If you cannot be a good motivator for the one you love then consider helping others in the hope that someone else will do the same for your family member.

My mother did exactly that. As a highly educated nurse, after a number of years, it became obvious that her love, while sustaining for both of us, was not a solution for her son. She realized the best outcome from what we had both been for her was for her to use her background in nursing to advocate for others. For a long time as a snowbird on Hilton Head, she volunteered on Sunday afternoons at our local chapter of the National Alliance for the Mentally Ill, facilitating their "Family to Family" class. For a few hours each week, off she went armed with a flip chart on an old school easel and her thick notebook full of handwritten reminders. She taught parents of other mentally ill children how to effectively love and cope with their sick family members. What a cool thing she did. I know it helped her get through many of the toughest times she had ever dealt with in her life.

A few years into my international job, I realized again that often the things we always wanted to happen in life come true, just in unexpected ways and at unexpected times. If you are not paying attention, you might not recognize these moments. With that, maybe now you better understand why I described my predecessors so fully in this memoir. I longed to be like them, and I fretted until I was 50 years old that my life had never really taken the right turn. My bipolarity was debilitating and frustrating for a long, long, time on many levels. I had all but given up on following in my family's footsteps. Somehow, however, I eventually did manage a semblance of the life I had always thought I would have, just maybe not how or when or how I had anticipated. Again, had I not been paying attention, I might not have realized that many of my long-given upon childhood aspirations of world travel and some kind of diplomatic role had actually come true.

On one occasion, I had the opportunity to fly to Washington for a day to attend a State Department meeting for J-1 visa vendors. After my earlier experiences on Capitol Hill, it was rewarding to be back on an official State Department visit, even if it was just a perfunctory meeting. Again, I was coming in through the side door, but life was still giving clues that I was headed in the right direction. Although on the flight home, I was at the edge of being too big for a coach seat on an airplane. I was mortified to have to ask flight attendants for a seat belt buckle extender.

Memories of those years of world travel are remarkable and will remain in my mind all my life, so I can't refrain from sharing a few of the highlights. Istanbul, with its magnificent Hagia Sophia, the Blue Mosque, its underground cistern, and the Grand Bazaar are all part of what so far has made it my favorite world city. Arriving for the first time in Istanbul over the Sea of Marmara was exhilarating, as was taking a ferry over the Bosporus Strait to cross from Europe to Asia. It's like an ancient New York City.

Turkey's 700-year-old Alayna Castle jutting out on a rocky peninsula overlooking the Mediterranean Sea took my breath away. So did Kyiv's Monastery of the Caves known for its buried monks whose sarcophagi do not decay. Rila Monastery in the mountainous Thracian region of Bulgaria, where Orthodox monks perfected the craft of painting religious iconography, was eye-popping, as were the gold-domed spires of the roofs of the summer palace in Adituyah, Thailand, where "The King and I" was set. Riding an elephant there was one thing that I thought would never happen to me. When I later shared a picture of me on the elephant with my mother, she inquired, "Was the elephant OK after that? They allow a guy your size on them?" Betsy was nothing if not direct.

And yet, like most of my best career opportunities, after almost five years, this one too would end in a firing. I was not getting better about how this felt. Relative to work experience on this team, I was a long-termer. The firm was known for running through employees, and my boss was tired of traveling with me. I had been in this position longer than many others. I'm sure that dinner in Manila where I twice broke into tears was the last straw.

By this time, I had moved from my waterfront condo overlooking Hilton Head's Broad Creek to an ocean-front one at the island's lands end. It had a view of the beach and the inlet to Calibougie Sound overlooking Daufuskie island and was just around the corner from Betsy & George's home. Another good set up for me.

By the spring of 2014, it was clear that my mother, age 78, was having serious health problems. For years, Betsy, George, and I, and even Connie beforehand, had volunteered every year at Hilton Head's

Heritage Golf Tournament, which Arnold Palmer had first made famous in 1969. Betsy had the coveted volunteer job for ladies of driving the pro golfers from the 18th green to the clubhouse in golf carts, while George and I served as marshals. Later, I was promoted to the announcers' committee, which meant that several of us would belt out the pros' names as they approached the ninth green. To avoid the traffic and shuttle buses around the tournament, we always rode our bikes to and from our posts. That year, it was obvious that this ride had become a huge effort for Betsy. So much so that one day, the usually lovely, pulled-together Betsy arrived home from the golf course looking like she had been run over.

George, my Aunt Nancy, her husband Ray, and I pulled a family intervention and confronted her about her health in her mother's sitting room just as we put Grandma's house on the market. I was still in the gaudy Scottish-themed uniform the announcers wore: red plaid knickers and knee socks, a flashy red blazer, a gold tie, and a traditional Heritage straw hat. We implored her to see a doctor. Mon's stage IV diagnosis came quickly in May, concurrent with the sale of my grandparents' house. George and Betsy left immediately to return to Ohio to start chemo. My relationship with my mother quickly evolved into something better than I think either of us had ever expected or imagined.

We had always been pretty darn close as a mother and son duo, despite the fact that tons of bipolar emotional baggage was the backdrop of our relationship. I had, however, learned early on that I could always make Betsy laugh. If we didn't actually see each other, we usually maintained a habit of a weekly phone call. But, from the day after her diagnosis until the day she died 15 months later, we spoke on the phone every day, with the exception of that trip to Manilla

At first, it was obvious she took my daily call because she knew I was the one who was worried and scared. Early on, I am sure this bugged her a bit, but she was patient about it, and after a few months, I knew my calls were touchstones for her. I could tell that she would wait for my calls with news to share, eventually even frequently ringing me up herself. For the first and only time in my life, I was becoming a go-to confidante for my mother. Given the history of our relationship, this was a surprisingly good lifetime result for both of us.

I learned a lot about family as my mother's illness progressed. There are patterns which occur in relationships that all families experience when a parent is dying. An important lesson I learned is one cannot judge how others react around sick people, and how they respond to death. It's an intensely individual personal journey that some face head-on, while others protect themselves often cloaked in stoicism. They purposely distance themselves to keep sadness, and perhaps their own personal demons at bay.

It's very common for one sibling to assume primary responsibility for their aging or dying parents' care. That is normal. There are lots of different reasons this happens in families. As with friendship, geography often has the most to do with it. In our case, I was a neighbor to my parents six months a year. I looked after their empty second home when they were in Ohio, while my siblings lived far away.

During my mom's illness, I found it fascinating but also disappointing to realize that my siblings and I each adopted differing core life values, despite having had the same upbringing in the same household. It's not that my core values are better than theirs, but that they're simply fundamentally different in a few ways. The understanding that George and Betsy's parenting had varying impacts on the three of us was something of a shock for me. I felt that my experience with my parents was a happy one. Although, I'm not sure that when my brother and sister look back on our childhood home they are buttressed by the memory of those happy times as a family in the same way that I am.

George was having just as many health problems as his wife at this point. He still suffered from his blood disorder, and was nursing two relatively new hips, He had also been knocked down the previous fall coaching Oakwood High School football on the sidelines. It resulted in breaking one of those recently replaced new hips. The Poor guy was carted off the sidelines in a golf cart discretely into Betsy's Lexus, and she drove him off to the hospital emergency room. As usual, this was followed by a few weeks in a rehab unit. This was also becoming a family pattern. After each hospitalization, whether for Betsy's cancer or George's orthopedic issues, we found ourselves with hours of time on our hands in various rehab units in the Dayton area. During these gigs, when one of my parents was in rehab and the other at home, they lovingly visited each other every day, twice a day. This was unbelievably difficult for them, both emotionally and physically. While it was sometimes a break for Betsy when she was at home and George was away at rehab. It was terribly isolating for dad when he was at home alone. All through Betsy's cancer treatment, my father had absolutely no clue that his wife's condition was terminal. She protected him from it, but her declining condition was perfectly clear. This isn't uncommon. When everyone else sees the handwriting on the wall, those closest to a dying patient often seem to be in a protective bubble and remain oblivious to the severity of condition.

The daily phone conversations and the many visits I made to and from Ohio brought our relationship as mother and son full circle. There was nothing we did not cover or share in that last year. "Do you have any regrets, Mom? Do you want a coffin, or do you want to be cremated? What kind of funeral would you like? What should I do about all the family finances without you in charge?" She was about to pass tremendous responsibility on to me that was way above my pay grade, but we were able to work through these problems together finally on the same page. Over the next several months together we planned and implemented her final wishes for all of us.

Over the next few years, when confronted with tough decisions as a caregiver for George or as a steward of his finances, I would ask myself "WWBD" as in "What would Betsy do?" In the same way many ask "WWJD," or "What would Jesus do?" …. Although I also considered Jesus in many life decisions for sure.

When she told me her only regret, it came as something of a surprise, but in the circle of her life, I realize it was not unlikely. "I would have preferred to remain a Protestant rather than to have converted to Catholicism when I married your dad." She said. "I would have been happy to go to St. Paul's Episcopal in Oakwood or Westminster Presbyterian downtown while your father took you kids to Holy Angels for Mass."

Who knew? As in everything else she did, my mom was a devoted, even devout Catholic. She never missed weekly mass or holy days. She even insisted upon extreme unction, the Catholic last rites when both she and George were on the fence. Five times I witnessed this ritual with my parents in hospital beds. Denouncing the devil in the presence of a priest when your mom and dad are facing their maker is something you do not easily forget. As far as the last rites go, we went 2 for five on final bedside sacraments, only two deaths in five times denouncing Satan. Not bad. In the end both of my parents defied major medical odds against them.

Mother even took to scripture to prepare for her passing, lunching, and visiting with our family priest, who had long since retired. He was, of course, the same priest who had set me up to live in the notorious attorney Joseph Keller's basement in Washington, D.C. with the Filipino guys. All the years later I realized these guys were the kind of students I would recruit for the American hospitality industry.

When I got the wee-hours phone call from a doctor in Ohio letting me know my mother passed away, I felt as if she had waved a wand in her ascent to heaven to give me the strength to assume her role as the head of our family. I suppose that might be a presumptuous thing to say, or follow through with even, but in our case, this was mandatory, no choice. My mom's death gave me the strength to do the multitude of things she did out of necessity as the working head of what she called "Stav, Incorporated." For general purposes, that phrase defined their three households and holdings. George for the most part did not participate in the family finances, but just about everything she did was for him. He was at the core. After her passing, George would become my charge. When my mother died, I stepped up to the plate. The increased responsibility was good for me.

We knew our mother's funeral would result in an outpouring of affection for her and our family in Ohio. As our relatives arrived in small groups in advance of the funeral that week, each evening we were elegantly entertained, fed, and comforted at the homes of Betsy and George's closest friends, also our own dear old friends having grown up with their children. The style in which my parents and grandparents and their crowd entertained and treated guests with polished silver, crystal, and putting their best food forward with elegant decor, menus, and service, all but gone with the wind. My nieces scoffed when we arrived at these kind and lovingly prepared evenings. They were offended by "the help" that our family friends employed, their regular bartenders, caterers, florists, and the like which one niece in particular perceived as servants. My Goddaughter was not shy about suggesting that she thought this was distasteful. Even when a casserole was sent home to us for us to dine together with just the family, favorite gals from local country clubs were sent to the house to cook, serve and clean up after us. How nice. As George would say, Betsy's funeral Mass and reception following in Dayton was a sell-out, standing room only crowd.

A second set of more private and discreet memorials would ensue in South Carolina where mom would be inurned in the family plot recently expanded for this very purpose. I was surprised to learn from our ever-faithful family friend and funeral director, who in his usual literal humor, George had nicknamed "Gravedigger," that the best way to send cremated human remains back to Hilton Head was with mother's urn wrapped in an old family lace table runner stuffed into her well used Vera Bradley overnight bag draped over my shoulder as a carry-on bag. When a random woman tried to cram her coat next to it in the airplane's overhead bin, I had to tell this stranger that it was my mother's ashes and to please be gentle. It was also awkward to sit at the Sbarro restaurant on my layover at Charlotte airport, probably eating something like a calzone, with my mother in a carryon bag in the seat next to me. It felt like we were hanging out together in a very surreal situation.

As I had promised Betsy, I relinquished my awesome ocean front condo and moved into the family house in Sea Pines to live with and care for my father. I would live in their second upstairs master bedroom. George was failing quickly. No one expected him to outlive Betsy for very long. As soon as he arrived from Ohio, I hired two shifts of home health workers, a beautiful very tall Jamaican woman named Barbara and her friend Thomasina who was from Costa Rica. They would share shifts arriving Monday through Friday mornings to make George's breakfast in time for me to head to a job I had taken at Marriott. They would leave when I returned home from work in time to prepare and serve George's dinner, which he eventually insisted I cook and serve as he was not a fan of the Caribbean flair our kind helpers would add to his meals.

This wore me out quickly, especially when I would wake to get ready for work to check on Dad, only to find him lying in bed in a pool of urine or with actual feces on Mother's new white carpeting and upgraded bedding that she had never gotten to use. Each time I got one messy crisis taken care of, another would occur. A wheelchair that had been discreetly tucked away was in frequent use at this point. A steady stream of physical therapists, occupational therapists, social workers, the whole nine yards, kept George engaged and gave him people to talk with on their recurring visits to the house. Betsy's Hilton Head friends took on the role of casserole queens for us.

I took him regularly to every specialist Mother had set him up with over the years- the oncologist, urologist, cardiologist, orthopedist, dentist, eye doctor, dermatologist. Finally, our family doctor explained the term "failure to thrive," and declared that Dad's condition, a domino effect of system failures coupled with the emotional loss of his wife, all meant that he was in trouble. His normally active social life and busy home were gone. All he did was watch Turner Classic Movies, the Golf Channel, and Fox News, all day.

Poor guy. He had just left behind an outpouring of hundreds of Ohio friends, not knowing he would never return to his home there. No one expected that the last time he would see any of his Dayton buddies would be at his wife's funeral. It was as if he had not only lost his wife, but his entire group of friends all at once. He was pretty good and mean, angry, and depressed, all with good reason. It was a sad time in life for both of us, yet I know my dad and I were grateful to have each other to go through it with. A first-time-ever antidepressant was prescribed for dad, and as with his son, the medicine had its intended effect. He remained notably cheerful all the way through his final years.

CHAPTER 13

FAMILY DYNAMICS

In November, I got a break from work and caregiving, and I traveled home to Dayton to participate in the events surrounding the 20th anniversary of the Dayton Peace Accords. I had continued my involvement in this process from Hilton Head. This was our Dayton Chamber of Commerce committee's finest coup. We finally got a President of the United States to attend one of our events. Bill Clinton would give a keynote address.

The night before the President's speech, we hosted an arrival party at Dayton's Carillon Historical Park. It was one of those rare, really fascinating nights in Dayton when the military and corporate brass turned out in our little midwestern town. I refer to that night and others like it since as Ambassador and General Palooza. Everywhere you turned, someone like Governor Bob Taft was standing right over your shoulder; you might then turn around and bump into a person with 4 stars on their epaulets. I didn't know who many of them were. I got to sit at the front row center table for the speech from the former POTUS the next day. This was the second time that I had been in the presence of Bill Clinton. Even as a self-proclaimed Nixon Republican, I have to admit that being in the very presence of our 42nd President is exhilarating. Despite all the tawdry drama, you know the minute he opens his mouth that he is one of the most brilliant and dynamic individuals on the planet.

That same evening, I was one of the hosts and emcee at a cocktail party at the Air Force Museum followed by a screening of the documentary "The Diplomat" directed by renowned filmmaker David Holbrooke, the son of the late Ambassador Richard Holbrooke, who brought Dayton back into the world spotlight. The committee was supposed to give me a list of questions, but they never came. Fortunately, at the last minute I was able to find a video on YouTube of Katie Couric moderating a screening of the same film, also with David Holbrooke, who it turns out was one of her long-time Today Show producers. I stole Katie Couric's script.

It was fun for me to introduce the panelists David Holbrooke and General Wesley Clark, a war hero who was a four-star general and had been Supreme Allied Commander in Europe. He had also served in both Vietnam and Kosovo, and in 2004 ran a formidable campaign in the Democratic presidential primary. This was the third time that I had attended an event in close quarters with General Clark. These people were beginning to recognize me, probably wondering who that big guy really is. My career as a "fake it 'til you make it" public diplomat was putting me in high cotton. I enjoyed paraphrasing Katie Couric and quizzing an actual world leader about his thoughts on NATO and Bosnia in front of a full Imax theater audience at Wright Patterson AFB that evening.

The final official event of the weekend was a cocktail reception at the Dayton Art Institute in it's Cloister. Then we moved into the museum's baroque-style auditorium, where I made a speech presenting the Dayton Peace Prize for Lifetime Achievement to Angelina Jolie and unceremoniously accepted the award on her behalf. "Ladies and Gentlemen, unfortunately, Ms. Angelina Jolie Pitt cannot be with us this evening as she is currently filming in Cambodia." It was a long shot that she would come to Dayton to accept, and years later, I am confident that she never knew she had been given the honor. This remains one of the funniest situations in my longtime random diplomatic career.

Let me leave no doubt though, The Dayton Peace Prize, which was given to commemorate the end of the war in Bosnia, is an esteemed honor, and it was previously accepted by Ambassador Holbrooke, President Clinton, and Archbishop Desmond Tutu. In another typical comical twist for me, given the added expense of President Clinton's visit, the committee was short on money to cast the cool bronze sculpture given to the honoree. In a pinch, I sponsored the casting of the trophy. I had it at home for the safekeeping of a future recipient for many years. It's an impressive contemporary artwork engraved with the name of a major film star and humanitarian and more than one Nobel laureate. It is quite a conversation starter, and last year, I was happy to pass it on for a permanent exhibit at the Dayton Peace Museum

Weeks later In January back home on Hilton Head, for the third time in five months, EMTs had to come to take George back to the emergency room. We had been to dinner the night before with his golf group, and someone was giving a Mardi Gras themed party in the club's ballroom. George was feeling good and, on our way out, he crashed the dance floor in his walker and danced with a masked woman who carefully spun him around a bit as the DJ played "YMCA!" He was so tickled about it, giggling on the way home in the car, even wondering if he could find out who she was to get her number. Such a simple thing gave him great joy.

His euphoria did not last. He woke me the next morning crying out to me upstairs that something was wrong and he couldn't move his right leg. I uncovered him to find a softball size contusion on his knee. I knew I could not get him out of bed myself. It was also obvious this meant hospitalization and rehab again, and the rehab facility we kept getting stuck into by hospital social workers was the pits. I had been trying all along to get him into a nicer facility but had been unable to accomplish any upgrades. My father's needs and increasingly challenging medical condition would consume the both of us for the next seven years.

In one episode early on in this process, I received a call from the nurses' station at the hospital. He had an adverse reaction to Benadryl. "Your father is in some kind of a daze, speaking gibberish. You need to get here right away." I dropped everything, then got a call while in the car on the way there. "Everything is OK," she said. "We have a nurse who has come in for her shift who is Catholic and explained that your dad is reciting the Nicene Creed in Latin." Unbelievably characteristic for this altar boy with dementia to rely on Jesus in his time of need. This would become another recurring theme in my dad's long goodbye, his lips moving, praying in his sleep a lot. The hospital's ultimate diagnosis was a condition called SAIDH: System Inappropriate Antidiuretic Hormone, also known as low salt. It is an increasingly common condition with symptoms that include inappropriate speech trending into turrets and an all-over body malaise.

Through these experiences, I began to rely on my Aunt Nancy and Betsy's widowed friends to help me figure out how to manage George. I had always been close to Nancy especially since she was my chosen in case of emergency contact during my original mental health hospitalization. She was good at helping me make tough calls. Among the best things I inherited from Betsy at this point were two of her best friends. Women I could call on for moral support and guidance. From the beginning, they told me it was OK to lie to George about the cost of his care. This enabled me to convince George that all of his expenses were covered by Medicare. For a while, he found this hard to believe. He had to convince himself to agree with me for his own protection. I knew if he ever found out the extent of his medical expenses, that he would go ballistic and insist on moving back home with me.

As for me, the agreed upon family plan was that I would live in George and Betsy's Sea Pines home until George eventually passed away, at which point I would sell it and split the proceeds with my siblings when George and Betsy's estates were finally settled. I don't think any of us expected that I would live in that house for as long as I did. The fringe benefits were pretty good including a gardening service, cleaning lady, pool service, and handyman at my disposal, not to mention two late model Lexus's in the garage. My knack for landing on my feet had me set up this time in another of my relatives' superlative homes close to the beach free of charge. Was I fortunate and entitled? Absolutely, but I also knew this was an answer to a "WWBD" question. Protecting their investment in that home, and its belongings while George was still alive nearby is where my mother would have wanted me. There was even financial precedent for it, as my family had kept my grandmother's home on the same Island for 21 years after she had died. Keeping a portion of their portfolio in real estate made sense.

No doubt, I also made effective use of having a nice big home, which was to share it with friends and fill it with family. I did both. I often hosted groups of friends for great parties there. Betsy had after all designed it for entertainment. I hosted family and had George delivered home from assisted living at Easter, Thanksgiving and Christmas, keeping the home fires burning for my dad, siblings, aunts, uncles, and cousins. My remaining at that house meant that the family experience in Sea Pines on Hilton Head continued uninterrupted as it had been since 1969. There was an upside in my latest upgraded accommodations for everyone in the family.

My role as George's surrogate in the handling of my parents' business was also increasing. By April, it was obvious that George would never return to our home in Dayton or Hilton Head. It was time to sell our last property in Ohio where we had lived for nearly 70 years. This started a snowball effect of work in unthinkable amounts. Of course, Betsy's homes were immaculate, the furnishings were all excellent quality, and there was an avalanche of valuable household chattel that we were not prepared to say goodbye to all at once.

To complicate matters, my parents' Hilton Head ocean-oriented house in which I was living was stuck in a thirty-year time warp. Everything was beautiful but dated and my folks having lived there a long time and the place had become cluttered. White carpet throughout, six rooms of wallpaper, and ugly slate green tile everywhere. It seemed ridiculous to bring the Ohio heirlooms to a house on Hilton Head where an update was 15 years overdue. I started to renovate my parents' Hilton Head home in preparation for all the belongings from the house we were listing in Ohio. I should have just donated all of it in the beginning, as most of it would make a pit stop in the Hilton Head garage then land in the hands of charities.

At this point I moved into a semi-retired period of my life, and at the young age of 53. I know there are those in my sphere of loved ones and friends who disapproved of this choice. I'll suggest that working for 33 years, nineteen jobs, nine firings, all while living with bipolar disorder was undoubtedly more stressful and difficult than it would be for those I knew who enjoyed entire lengthy, professional careers, working through age 65 and beyond. At least at this point, I did not need more of the job firings, stops, starts, and restarts I had continued to go through. I was due and ready for a break. I realized a few years later that my need for space at this time had more to do with bandwidth than just being over it with my career. I learned my bipolar brain has only so much to give before I wear it down. Understanding my limits now, good self-protective instincts kick in and help me make good life decisions, at least I think so. I did not have enough in me to work, care for my father, manage real estate, taxes, and the multitude of my late mom's responsibilities had turned into something like a full-time job for me.

Relative to my mood at this point, it had been as many as 10 years since I had taken any medication for the mood disorder, other than during my years in international travel. Then, my doctor had prescribed Xanax to manage the long flights on which I could not use the C-PAP machine I relied upon for sleep apnea. I could no longer sleep without the whirring machine for fear of stroking out overnight at home alone. At this point I had taken Xanax increasingly on an "as needed" basis. There were, perhaps three times in that ten-year period, I had used a quick Prozac fix to shake a bad mood. Other than that, as a young retiree mourning the loss of my mother to whom I had been extremely close, my moods were pretty happy and stable.

I was in fact doing well. But even as I lived alone, I began to notice a few noteworthy changes in my personality. My triggers were twofold: first I was mourning. This was my first real experience with a major loss, and I put a tremendous amount of pressure on myself when it came to managing both George's care and finances. I'll be damned, there was no way I was going to screw it up on my watch.

When triggered, I developed a quick temper. I would get flash angry at inappropriate moments, usually in the throes of the seemingly unending task of continuing to go through volumes of family possessions that I had packed in Ohio, then needed to find a place for in South Carolina. I could break out in a long list of creative cuss words that would make a sailor blush. I was not above smashing something or throwing something against a wall or in a pile to blow off steam. In the beginning, my outbursts would scare Barbara, George's former caregiver who had become my weekly housekeeper, which was one of the best decisions I ever made. After a while, she got used to my outbursts and took me in like family, thank goodness. It was especially important to me not to trash my parents' house the way I had my bachelor pads. I had gone from being the slovenly "Oscar Madison" in the "Odd Couple," to the nitpicking housekeeper "Felix Unger!" An occasional dose of Xanax did the trick to calm me down when my combination of depression and anxiety presented in the form of anger.

This time, as in previous major mood swings, the outward evidence of my emotional state could not have been more obvious. In advance of Betsy's funeral, knowing it would embarrass even Betsy in her grave if I arrived fat to her funeral, I lost 50 or 60 pounds. But the year after her passing, and in the following next couple of years, I would expand and expand again to ogre-like proportions at 350 pounds. I looked like Shrek looming over people in photographs. Of course, when I looked at myself in the mirror, I saw a different guy altogether. I only saw the truth in rare group photos. I had to buy triple extra-large clothes and was up to a size 44 waist and 21-inch neck. Pretty grotesque. I knew what I was doing but would continue to let this slide. George referred to my size as "A real attention getter."

That not everyone was as enamored with me as I had always been with myself was becoming a pattern. I would joke about myself, often even referring to myself as an "acquired taste" when introduced to new folks. After all, in my condition, I could be a sight to behold. It takes some confidence for really heavy people to try to feel their best going out in public, especially for single people to show up at things alone. I knew what it felt like to be invisible, which is not easy with my size and personality.

Occasionally over the years, when I had dropped significant weight, I'd be taken aback when people would look me in the eye in public at the grocery store, at a bar, or waiting in a line. Most normal people are flattered to be checked out this way, but whenever this happened when I was thinner, it made me remember what it felt like to never get anything more than a side glance when I was overweight. Even worse would be the occasional disapproving look from people judgmental of the overweight. In the meantime, I wore the best looking big and tall clothing I could find and made it a habit. It would be a couple of years before I would hear the term "binge eating disorder" associated with the rest of my psychosis, but when this did finally roll around, it was like another light bulb going off, just like when I got my bipolar diagnosis.

As I have finally begun to share these last few years, so much has happened that I had to scroll through my phone's camera roll to remember the order in which everything has gone down. I'm glad to note that, as I scroll backwards from the present day to 2016, a key running theme of all my photos are pictures of George. During that period, in good times and bad, we became bosom buddies, especially as his dementia and isolation became deeper.

As often as I could, I stopped in for visits with loot from errands he would request, bringing dated items for old men like Old Spice, Aqua-Velva aftershaves, or Vitalis man's hair grease. Often, we would head to dinner on Saturday at the club with the golf group or to lunch with his Tuesday group at Hilton Head's popular Reilley's Bar and Grill. I'd sling the wheelchair or walker in and out of the back of his Lexus and off we would go. It provided Dad real peace of mind that his car was still in the garage at home. "Have you had it serviced? How's the oil level? What pressure do you have on the tires? You need to take this car to get it washed, please!"

George loved pizza, but this was one item lacking on the nursing home's menu. Every once in a while, he would crave it. So, from time to time, we would head out together in search of the perfect slice of pizza. We hit every pizza joint on Hilton Head. After about three bites at each place, Dad would announce, "This pizza sucks." It became a running joke between us. We never did find what he wanted. Marion's pizza in Dayton, Ohio, is hard to beat.

Turning on the car radio when we were tooling around together was touchy, as about any familiar song that came on would remind him of Betsy. He could easily break into tears telling me how much he loved her, missed her, all the things that she did for him, the way she helped him, all of the tough decisions she made for them, so he didn't have to. Almost every time he would express his own guilt saying that he wished he had hugged or kissed her more or been nicer to her. In reality, he was all of these things to her. She adored him. Never was there any time, at least that any of us ever knew, that Betsy had ever suffered any hurt or disappointment from George. They enjoyed a true two people united as one kind of marriage. As their son, it was a blessing and an honor to witness.

It was at this point that dementia, the long goodbye about which Ronald Reagan had so poignantly written, would become a lifetime milestone for both my father and for me. The breaking point in Dad's mind came during Hurricane Matthew in October 2016. George's fellow residents and the staff of the entire nursing home as well as many from the larger adjoining retirement community, about 250 seniors, were evacuated *en masse* on chartered buses inland to Augusta, Georgia, to a nice high-rise Sheraton Hotel. As good luck would have it, I had also evacuated with friends to Augusta. This was a real bonus for both of us. I knew he was safe and could even check in on him.

The scene of the whole retirement community's removal to a high-rise hotel was a riot. The lobby was packed. Its' walls and even its hallways were bordered by row upon row of really old people in their wheelchairs. The ballroom was converted into a temporary dining hall with long rows of tables. Residents played bridge, gin rummy, or sang at a piano. Other hotel guests, also displaced and evacuated, were in and out of the lobby in a steady stream with their pets. It looked like the hotel was hosting a dog show. Every television in sight was blaring college football at top volume. The activities staff even planned their regular seated yoga exercise classes and bus outings to the mall and other Augusta attractions. It was a scene right out of the movie "Cocoon!" George was having a ball socializing. He enjoyed having a roommate for the weekend, a new audience for his Carolina football stories. He was giddy.

It would be five days before Hilton Head Island was reopened for residents to return. Our island was the epicenter of Matthew's damage. The devastation was gut wrenching. The job that first responders did to make re-entry safe was heroic. For the next several months just about every road on our 12-mile-long Island was lined on either side with 10-12-foot-tall piles of stacked up logs. Tens of thousands of trees were lost. Key harbors were damaged, and in one case, destroyed. Everything was a mess. Our family home was spared, even as many neighbors had their homes partially or in some cases, completely destroyed.

George's right mind was collateral damage. The buildup to leaving for evacuation and the trip to and from Augusta confused him badly. He would never again be quite sure of where he was. Sometimes he'd think he was in Ohio, or in Augusta. He started to refer to his assisted living suite as his hotel or hospital room. It was even harder during our phone calls when he would think he was at the Carolina football training table getting ready for a game, or worried that he had missed coaching Oakwood football practice. After a while, he would forget that Betsy had died, and would ask me where she was or what she was up to. The saddest of these nuggets came the day when he called to tell me that he had heard Betsy's new husband had passed away, and that he wanted to know if she was all right, figuring she would be upset that her new husband had died. Poor George in his demented mind had concluded that Betsy must still be alive and had left him for another man. I quickly learned the technique of re-directing conversations with him to easy topics like his meals, the weather, or sports on television.

I expect some readers might be thinking I've gone on too long a tangent on my father's slide into dementia and my experience with it. So, I'd like to make it clear why these shares are important. The reality is, as many times as I was saddened witnessing his mental and emotional decline, I was frequently equally awed at beautiful full circle life moments he experienced because of his dementia. In nearly the same way I personally find beauty in the human condition in my bipolar brain, there were beautiful occurrences in my father's demented mind.

Perhaps this is how we should look at all mental health problems, from the outside in. Very cool things happen even in broken minds of all kinds. I was not disappointed that my father's frequent out of touch with reality alternate delusional universe placed him back on the football field in his heyday, on road trips with long missed old golf buddies, even worried that he was late for practice, or that he missed an important sales call with his brain harkening back to his days as a successful businessman. Often these hours long even days long delusions put him in a better place than his current reality as an extremely lonely widower and a very social individual confused and bored to distraction in a ground hog day lifestyle and limited environment in nursing care. I was proud of how he made the best of it. He took his life seriously still motivated to achieve and make other people smile.

CHAPTER 14

THE LONG GOODBYE

Dad's dementia expressed itself in fixations. This included a fixation on the telephone and calling me, often as much as a dozen times a day. I couldn't keep myself from answering at least half these calls, even knowing I would go through the same conversations every day, all day. "Where's my car, I drove it yesterday and left the keys in it," he would tell me. "Where do I live? Where do you live? Did Mom die?" Again and again, he'd wonder, "Where's my car?" Often, he would call to tell me, "My brother and those bad guys came over here, threw me into the trunk of my car, took me to the country club, beat me up, and took all my money, those bastards!" The plots from the various Turner Classic movies he watched all day would become reality in his mind. The same bad things happened to him, repeatedly.

It became evident that I was not the only person George was calling. I learned that he would call the nurses' station, security, or even occasionally 911 from his room if I did not pick up the telephone when he called me to check on his car. From time to time, they would have to literally pull the plug from the phone in his room. He would get angry that his phone was "broken", but after a few days without it, his fixation would be reset, for maybe a week.

Professionals, doctors, and friends would always try to explain that his anxiety and fixations, his internal emotional battles and other dementia-related symptoms were harder on me as a caregiver than it was for him to experience life in this way. I have trouble believing this is true. I had the intellectual capability to compartmentalize these situations. I developed the skill of being able to sort of put the emotional burden of witnessing my dad's progression in a box and could put it on a shelf. I tried three times to get him into a terrific Hilton Head brain health and memory care program called Memory Matters, but he refused it eventually, swearing at me over it, embarrassed that we thought he needed it, feeling stigmatized.

When he retired full-time years ago, George had taken an interest in painting, and even took a few classes. At home at Hilton Head while Betsy would be working away in the house, he would occasionally get out his paints and set up a blanket and a canvas on the trunk of Betsy's car in the garage. With a paint brush in one hand and a lit cigar in the other, George would paint images he had collected from magazine clippings. "Don't you dare bring that nasty cigar into this house!" She would scold him.

His primitive landscapes and still life paintings were really pretty good. Betsy had framed and hung a number of them. The nursing home activities coordinator and I conspired for a long time to get him to paint again, but he refused. Luckily, consistent with his nature as a very social person, George was a pretty good joiner of activities planned by the staff. He faithfully attended group exercise programs, and he almost never missed the weekly Mass in the activities room.

When he lost his wallet in his little bedroom the third time with all of his identification and the small amount of cash I would give him, I gave up replacing it. Not having a full wallet was emasculating for him. He also lost his UNC letterman's college ring, a real beauty, and a treasured possession. I felt awful for him. He had had such a comfortable ride his whole life and was reduced to a small bedroom suite and that was a mountain for him to manage.

This was just before Christmas, and after a few years of caring for him, I realized his emotions followed a pattern. Dad's failure to thrive almost always coincided with the holidays, and in the spring in May and June. George and Betsy were married at Christmas, and as a widower, every time the ornaments came out, it would make him miss her so much he would become distraught. The same would happen when their birthdays rolled around. He would deteriorate every year like clockwork at these times. Through all of this, we still had been able to get out together to the club, his lunches at Reilley's, or out in search of the perfect pizza slice. We would have holiday meals at home or at Sea Pines Country Club, occasional dinners out with Aunt Nancy and Uncle Ray.

We continued Procrit treatments for myelodysplastic syndrome, George's blood disorder. His cancer was all but in remission for a few years with only the need for a blood transfusion once or twice a year. Betsy used to laugh with friends about Dad's transfusion days. The fresh blood made him feel like superman and she would plan dinners out with friends in advance on these nights knowing George would be feeling his best. Funny, my grandmother's good days during her passing from painful multiple myeloma were her chemo days when she could have her Cutty Sark and soda with Percocet at happy hour. In the same vein, George and Betsy would kick their heels up on his transfusion days. Good people in my book! They really knew how to live.

Occasionally, on my trips back to Ohio while Betsy was sick, I would run into my old boss and buddy Paul at Dayton's Carmel's bar. In past years, I have sometimes met various friends there during my rare visits home. Now, the trips had evolved into rather frequent ones. It had been nearly ten years since Paul and I had spoken. Not long our reunion in Dayton, he stopped on Hilton Head with his girlfriend Angie. They had been visiting one of his twin boys who was now a student at College of Charleston. Three of us had a good time on Hilton head for a few days, hanging out poolside at home or on the beach nearby. Not long afterwards, they announced that they were getting married in June at Key West, and Paul asked if I would give the toast at their wedding reception. Unexpected but ok.

In Key West I stayed at the old school Casa Marina Waldorf Astoria on my own, separate from the small band of about 20 family members and friends who stayed at the wedding venue, Key West's Pier House Resort a mile or two away. The wedding was a good time. Paul's twin sons, my old pals from when I managed their dad's parking company came together as their father's two best men. My speech was not my best work. Awkwardly, I even referenced the twins' mother, the groom's ex-wife, who had sent me to check on him as many fifteen years prior during their ugly divorce.

On the heels of that, as a follow up to my visit in Dayton for the Peace Accords Anniversary, I went to Washington, D.C. to support our Bosnian counterparts, the American Society for Bosnia Herzegovina. Their annual gala that year honor President Clinton, so a pair of us from Dayton decided it would be fun to go to a black-tie function in the Capitol thinking we might get another chance for a brush with the President. It was a nice getaway for me. I spent two days by myself in my old neighborhood of Alexandria, Virginia. For the next two nights I moved across the Potomac and stayed at the historic Mayflower Hotel, just around the corner from the event's venue, a great old mansion called the Whitmore House. An Embassy Row Mansion private club which inside had the look and feel of the state rooms at the White House.

When we arrived, we were delighted to find out that President Clinton would actually attend and make a speech. Even better, I had sponsored a table as we were acting as an unofficial Dayton Delegation, so we would be seated at table number one at the dais right next to the honorees. Too much fun for me to be dressed in a tux in this environment. The list of dignitaries I could chat up at the nearly full table I had sponsored was a hoot. On my right was a beautiful woman who was the Ambassador to the US from Kosovo, while on my left was a nice woman who was the former US Ambassador to Lesotho, as well as her husband who had a long diplomatic career and had served as an ambassador to a couple of different countries. Our other table mates included our friends on the board of the American Society for Bosnia Herzegovina as well as General Wesley Clark, the Supreme Commander of Allied Forces in Europe who I previously introduced in Dayton, and who I think was annoyed by me. One person did not show, so there was an empty seat at our table.

It was thrilling again to be in a room at arm's length from Bill Clinton as he spoke. The plated meal was difficult as we were supposed to eat during the speeches, but it was hard to do eyeball to eyeball with the 42nd President as he spoke just a few feet away from us. I could tell the beautiful young Ambassador from Kosovo next to me was also struggling with what to do about the food in front of her under these circumstances.

Usually, the expectation is that the President would depart following his speech in a bubble of Secret Service, but it seems he was having a good time, so decided to stay and hear the other honorees' speeches. He stood with his agents leaning against the wall adjacent to our table for a few minutes until he noticed our empty seat. We were all silently flabbergasted when he sat down and joined our group for the next hour and a half. We shook hands, said hello, and shared some small talk between speeches. This was too damn funny. How could it be that a guy like me could end up hanging with the former President of the United States, in recurring situations even.

The evening was one standing ovation after another, and each time I got up, my ill-fitting rental tux and cummerbund would have to be readjusted. In the course of rustling my clothes as we stood clapping, I kept bumping elbows with one of the honorees at the table next to me.

He was a general I had never heard of before who was being honored for his work in his retirement promoting land mine detection dogs. His speech was one of the most exciting rip-roaring go get 'em motivators I had ever heard. It was great! As the speeches were ending and we were on our feet brushing shoulders hopefully just one last time, I turned to him and spoke. "One more standing ovation like this and I think my pants are going to fall down." The lady Ambassadors on either side of me broke out in laughter, as did the General.

I headed home to Hilton Head thinking I should find out more about that guy. I learned at the click of a button that I was joking around with General Gordon R. Sullivan, yet another four-star general, the Chief of the Army, a member of the Joint Chiefs of Staff, and finally the acting Secretary of the Army. The US Army Band even had a march dedicated to him, his own national anthem, "The Architect of Victory." This guy was a national hero, and I was cracking jokes. I was so inspired by him I would participate in his organization, the Marshall Legacy Institute, which is the modern-day evolution of the Marshall plan to rebuild a ravaged Europe after WWII. Pretty exciting stuff for a guy like me who once yearned for a professional experience with people like this.

Around Thanksgiving of that year, I was semi-retired for a few years, and eager to reinvent in some kind of a professional endeavor involving income, but I had been having trouble pulling the trigger and was not moving forward. I consulted with my therapist and my personal physician, and both encouraged me to consider finally trying meds for my mood disorder. After years of refraining from the use of meds other than Xanax, darn if they didn't come around prescribing good old Prozac. It was, however, my idea. I wasn't exactly thrilled with the idea of long-term antipsychotics. Still, I still was having trouble motivating the switch between semi-retirement and reinvention, and figured I would try again to see if some medicine would help me focus. A little bit of a rookie error here in my selfcare. I should have gone to a psychiatrist for a prescription, not my general practitioner. I likely would have discovered a more sophisticated prescription.

In December of 2018, I returned to Dayton to dedicate a new venue honoring my mother at the just completed Miami Valley Hospital South Orthopedic Wing. I was on the uptake of Prozac during this visit. I had forgotten about the side effects I had experienced more than once during the uptake of Prozac, I was restless, having flop sweats, wild dreams, and it was obvious I was experiencing pressured speech. All of the reasons I had given up Prozac in the first place. I would give it up quickly, sticking with the occasional Xanax at happy hour. Of course, I would continue to self-medicate with pot.

It was a picture of me with old family friends at the Gala the hospital foundation hosted for Betsy's ribbon cutting that was the final straw. With a family of four, two of them on either side of me, I looked about the size of the car they had come in on. The time had come for me to really do something about my weight. I had begun collaborating for a year with a personal trainer at a gym on Hilton Head, but I had barely budged a pound. I had been aching for an actual vacation and had been searching for quite a while for just the right trip to take on my own but couldn't come up with it. I was finally encouraged by my trainer and other friends to try a yoga retreat to kick off a weight loss effort, so in January I headed to Esterillos Oeste, Costa Rica with a group of mainly ladies and a couple of husbands dragged along for the ride. This was really a communal beach vacation on the theme of yoga and vegan food. The trip's expense gave me the motivation to stick with a program of fitness and nutrition. On a side note, during this trip, I also learned that for many women "yoga retreat" is code for slipping away for a facelift or other cosmetic procedure.

There would be another quick trip to Washington for the annual gala of The American Society of Bosnia Herzegovina. This would be fun, as the year before I had attended carrying all that weight. This time, however, I had dropped about 75 pounds. The kickoff to my weight loss program had been a big success. I followed my itinerary from the previous year, enjoying a couple of days in both Alexandria at my favorite Alexandrian Hotel and crossed over into DC for a couple of nights at the Mayflower. I was also eager to experience some culture while I was there by myself, so I booked a ticket to a National Symphony Orchestra concert at the Kennedy Center. I figured why not. I had not been to a symphony orchestra concert for over 20 years and having been dragged to concerts frequently by my mother as a boy, I enjoy classical music as much as the next guy. I was shocked when I arrived at the Kennedy Center to learn that the conductor had fallen ill, so the performance had been canceled at the last minute. I'm just a hick from Ohio, I thought, but haven't these people ever heard "The show must go on?"

Unphased, I went to the ticket office and found I could upgrade my ticket and catch the world famous Russian Mariinsky Ballet company perform "Le Corsair" in three acts. Frankly, I had never heard of the famous Russian dance company or the ballet they would perform. I don't even really like ballet. I ended up with a great seat in a box, and when I arrived in the lobby outside of it, I was surprised to read a plaque expressing that the box in which I was sitting had been dedicated in the memory of Robert F. Kennedy by Mrs. and Mrs. Sergeant Shriver. I would get to sit in RFK's box in the Kennedy Center Opera House right next to the Presidential Box. The music was beautiful and the scenery first rate, but I have to admit the plot about shipwrecked pirates and a tribe of alluring Amazon siren ladies was more than hard to follow. I slept slumped over in the Kennedy family seats for most of the performance.

CHAPTER 15

UNEXPECTED WHIRLWIND

I'd returned to Hilton Head in time to don my uniform for the Heritage golf tournament. I had to have about 30 inches taken all the way around but I was still swimming in it. While I had been in Dayton for the hospital dedication, I had reached out to my old friend Paul's ex-wife Kathy. Six or seven years before, her whole family had moved pretty much *en masse* from Dayton to Charleston two hours north of Hilton Head, and Kathy had recently followed them. Since she was new to the area, and an old friend not far away, I thought it would be fun to get together. After a few phone calls back and forth over the course of a few months, she agreed to come down to Hilton Head for the golf tournament. Kathy was a hard-working single mother whose career had evolved very successfully. She had worked her way up to a position as a high-powered globetrotting IT executive, who, by the way, is a stunningly beautiful blond.

I had the final round as a day off from my shifts announcing the players arrivals on the 9th green, but still wore my uniform for entertainment's sake. I bought us box seats in a new Charleston Club venue on the 18th green. We walked the course, Kathy bought a jacket in a shop at Harbourtown. We ran into a few friends and sat in the sun in our box seats just the two of us. The new Charleston Club seats had yet to catch on, and we had pretty much had our own private catered spot to watch Japan's Satoshi Kadaira win the Heritage at 12 under in a playoff.

At this point at 55 years of age, I had all but given up the prospect of marriage in my life. I had given love a serious chance a few times, but none of my previous relationships had gotten over the finish line. Over the course of the past couple of years caring for my father, I had spent a lot of time online checking out things like "Top 10 cities for single people to retire," knowing that Hilton Head, especially at the far end of Sea Pines, where I was living, was not a great spot as a forever home for a single man with no family in the neighborhood, particularly one who wasn't really a golfer or a boater for that matter. I pictured what my life might look like after George passed away. I could see myself in Florida, Charlotte, Raleigh-Durham, or Atlanta. I even looked into Las Vegas. I was game for a new life in a community where a guy like me and his dog could get around and make some decent connections in a new town. I had also lived alone for a very long time and was aware that my mood disorder was a challenge to any relationship. I figured I was one of those guys who maybe just shouldn't get married after all and was OK with it, and was planning for my future alone.

Instead, two months later after a whirlwind romance, Kathy, and I were engaged in a big family event produced by my future sister-in-law at the lovely new Hotel Bennett in Charleston. We flew Kathy's other twin son in from Cincinnati where he was attending engineering school at UC. The boys could hardly believe their mother suddenly getting remarried after 17 years, and were having a little trouble getting used to the idea. Even though they had known me since they were toddlers, the last time they had seen me was at 350 pounds at their dad's Key West wedding the previous summer. They had yet to see the transformation of my frame, for by this time I had lost nearly 100 pounds. Things happened so quickly I had to make phone calls to ask the twins and Kathy's mother for her hand. The expense of that weekend blew me away, especially the engagement ring. I was okay with it, though, knowing I had gotten off easily as a bachelor all those years.

Just to make sure you caught that before it goes by too quickly. First surprise, I married in an expected whirlwind. As it happened, I was the pretty much the best man at my wife's ex-husband's wedding when he got married after their divorce. I had been his high school football coach, and later I worked for him. I have known my new 21-year-old twin stepson's since they were babies. George had later been their own high school coach. Kathy and I had met in 1974 in fifth grade. She was one of the best girl singers and I one of the best guys in our class, so we sang all of the way through school together, up to starring in the aforementioned South Pacific production which still provides fun memories for both of us.

I should take a minute here to share some of my thoughts and feelings about Kathy. As I try to put some of these feelings into words, the first things I come up with are sensory. Spritzed with her designer fragrances, she always smells wonderful in a way that makes a guy want to wallow in it, and she never fails to look beautiful, almost always perfectly and elegantly put together. She knows what looks best on her and is a head turner every time she walks in a room. She takes my breath away whenever she makes an entrance. From the beginning, I knew she was my biggest fan. Given our history, she understood me in a way that no other woman ever had. This was eye opening, comforting, relaxing, no pretense or pressure, a kind of turn on I had never experienced. She is a foot shorter than I am, with classic good looks and a curvy figure that as long as I have known her, she has fallen somewhere between buxom and Rubenesque and has recently evolved towards petite. To me, she might as well be the Mona Lisa.

For our second date on Hilton Head, we went to Harbourtown and rented jet skis. I had never been on one before, and I could not get over how cute she was in a bikini, a cool pair of Ray Bans, a lifejacket, and a ball cap. I could not take my eyes off her as she zoomed around on the water with her ponytail flying in the wind behind her. I realize now this was the moment I fell in love with her for certain, as I sat on an idling jet ski in an early spring bloom of millions of harmless jellyfish in the Calibougie Sound in the shadow of the Harbourtown Lighthouse. Afterwards, we shared a snow cone. It was great.

We went to dinner that night at Harbourtown's classic CQ's restaurant, which my grandparents had often enjoyed as much as 50 years ago. I never felt more like a whole man than I did that night proudly walking into the dining room with her on my arm. We cuddled poolside at my parents' old home in the moonlight that night, already talking about a future together. This kind of romance blew me away.

Kathy was renting a cool loft condominium in Charleston's French Quarter at Queen and Bay Streets, a spectacular address on one of Charleston's most photographed blocks. It was what George would call a short seven iron away from the city's landmark Pineapple Fountain. There were great views of the contemporary Ravenel Bridge over the Cooper River, across to Patriots Point and the USS Yorktown, and Mt Pleasant where Kathy's mother lived. For the next year, we could enjoy the best of both worlds in the amazing Holy City of Charleston and on Hilton Head. My introduction to this great southern town with Kathy and her family was some of the most fun I had ever had in my life.

It was a lot to absorb, but spending time in Charleston with Kathryn and getting to know the city was not a chore. I'd be lying if I didn't cop to the fact that I was a little intimidated by some of the new people I was meeting in my in-laws' sphere in Charleston. The level of wealth, from some really old prestigious southern families, could be daunting. All of them, however, couldn't have been nicer or more welcoming to me. It was exciting.

The buildup to our wedding was literally too much fun. To be honest, I had been ramping up my use of Xanax. I was not unaware that my diet regimen of pounding Xanax and coupling it with vodka in the evening, had become an easy habit to make, but a hard one to break. I'm sure the relaxation provided by it appeased my fixation on food. I had continued to lose a lot of weight and after six months, I had lost too much weight too quickly, 120 pounds! Even my gym friends were telling me I had taken it a tad too far. I was looking thin as a rod for the first time in my entire life. My personal trainer, Pete, a former Navy search and rescue diver and a great guy who was developing into one of my best friends pointed out a never-before-seen ribcage on my body. I had even developed some abs. The biggest transformation was in my face, which had unfortunately begun to even cave in a little, no longer supported by a layer of fat and fluid. Oh well.

My old friend Pam came to visit us for a short week on Hilton Head. She is the one who had taken me to Kettering hospital the night I had really wigged out more than 20 years ago. Pam had left Dayton for Alabama about that time, and this was a long overdue reunion. I was excited that she would get to spend some time with my fiancé Kathryn. Pam was a couple of years into a journey with Parkinson's disease; it was tough to watch someone I love going through it. But more than a year later, Kathy and I joke together that Pam is not welcome back, for it seems that every time Pam is around, I end up in a mental hospital or rehab. Kathy and I got good and tanked one night during Pam's visit. I was sailing on red wine, weed, and Xanax. I learned that night that my fiancé could be what they call a real "woo hoo girl" if she was overserved. Mind you, this isn't a complaint!

The following morning with Pam in the kitchen, Kathy and I sat out by the pool together and recapped the previous night over coffee. Immediately, we decided upon a drug and alcohol-free marriage. At my own suggestion, I signed up to go to Sierra Tucson to get clean. I decided I would give up pot, the prescription, and quit vaping tobacco, which had replaced my beloved Marlborough Lights years ago. It didn't occur to either of us that suddenly picking up and heading to Arizona for rehab was a little extreme given the level of my habits, and that I was sure my biggest problem was only marijuana, as I wasn't addicted to the Xanax. I just had the propensity to enjoy it too much.

Within a week, off to Arizona I flew, committed to cleaning up my act. My stay at Sierra Tucson was surprising on a few levels. I couldn't get over how many of the patients I met there were back for their second, even third attempt at rehab. Many of the people in treatment in our group even had long friendships as a result of previous visits together at the same facility. I wondered why they would keep coming back to the same facility if the program hadn't worked for them in the first place.

In pre-arrival conversations with their admission teams, I had explained that I was coming to dry up as well as explore with therapists the concept of concurrent diagnosis of bipolarity and drug abuse with marijuana. My goal was to clean out my head, re-immerse myself in a curative environment, and basically have a mental health tune up before getting married. I had chosen the wrong facility to make this happen. Instead, after detoxing just one night from weed and my prescription narcotics, to my consternation, they re-prescribed my same old Depakote, Prozac and Ativan cocktail, and set me up with the rest of the "Twelve Steppers." I had privileges so I could get my cell phone and iPad out of lock up twice a day to make calls to Kathy and George. I lifted weights, swam laps, took long walks in the trails around the campus, sat in on group therapy, and took all of the required classes in their auditorium. I had signed up and paid a bundle and was all in on it. The first, second, and third day passed, but I had yet to see a psychiatrist. I was confident, adamant, and persistent. I wanted to meet with a board-certified, properly credentialed, able to prescribe medicine physician and would not settle for anything less. They placated me first with a retired army psychologist, whom they tried to pass on as an MD. They did this a second time the following day with a lady psychologist who had a streak of purple dye running through her hair. In the course of our hour together, she confided to me that she was also a regular pot smoker. She made me promise not to tell anyone or she would lose her job. Red flag city for a patient I thought.

About nine o'clock in the evening, I attended the obligatory men's dorm meeting. I was kind of surprised that our men's group had class officers and facilitators, though I'm not sure if these guys were nominated by the group or singled out by caseworkers. With the exception of the 12-step theme, these meetings before lights out were like the old Monday chapter meetings at my old fraternity house at Allegheny. All of the patients were given a nickname, and every night a few got up and gave their stories and tributes. When good news was given or someone deserved praise, all the guys would snap their fingers in unison instead of clapping. I respected it, but this was not the vibe I needed in my wellness journey at this point, and after four days I had yet to see a psychiatrist.

"I hear you're thinking about checking out." Our dorm's class president said, sitting next to me in the cafeteria.

"If I don't see an actual psychiatrist today, I'm out of here." I explained. I was promised a meeting with the head doctor in charge that afternoon.

"Well, if I don't see you again, would you like to know the nickname the guys came up with for you?" he asked.

"Sure, why not." I chuckled.

"It's Thurston Howell the Third." He told me.

Great. The eccentric millionaire castaway from Gilligan's Island played by Jim Backus. In my defense I had paid extra and was the only guy in our group that had a private room. Plus, I dressed the best I could knowing at least for me that the way you look is the way you feel. I also had a lot of new, more expensive clothes because they looked pretty good on my strong thin frame. But Thurston Howell III, ugh. This really sounded like my old fraternity days when my pledge class nickname was Charles Emmerson Winchester the boorish Bostonian Snob on the 70's series M*A*S*H. Oh well, I am the product of an old school patrician upbringing and the beneficiary of a decent amount of privilege, and there is by nature an old school aura of it about me. I imagine over the years I have played this up intentionally, maybe to give the impression I'm a man of substance whether it's true or not. One thing I'm sure about, I almost never have the emotion of feeling better in any way than anyone else in a room. I still remember a song from early Catholic catechism. We were taught Disney's "Wonderful World of Color Spectrum Song" to teach us about diversity, and it has always stuck with me. Still, with the upheaval in today's culture over race relations and diversity, being tagged as an elitist makes some sense, but it makes me cringe a bit at the same time. I own it, but I will also share that I am a firm believer that with any privilege comes great responsibility. I have tried to make that a guiding principle in my life.

After I was told that their psychiatrist would not be able to see me that afternoon after all, I kept my word and checked out. When I called to say I was on my way home, Kathy, our loyal cleaning lady, Barbara, and my handyman and household helper, Geoff, could not have been more shocked. "You can't come home now!" Kathy cried. The three of them were in the middle of a project for me and were not ready for the reveal. They were also concerned I would arrive home in a pile after unsuccessful treatment.

While I was gone, I had given Kathy permission and a reasonable budget to purchase a new bedroom suite for us. She was creeped out sleeping in George and Betsy's big old four poster bed that I had shipped down from Ohio and installed in the Hilton Head poolside master bedroom that we had made our own. It was a fair call. No bride at any stage of life should have to sleep in her husband's parents' bedding.

Furthermore, we had yet to decide whether we would stay and live in the family home until George died, as had been my intention as a bachelor. Living together in Charleston was still on the radar. We even considered moving back to Dayton together. George, our dog Blackie, and the thresholds of my willingness to spend were all important considerations, and we were leaning on pushing that decision until after our wedding, which was fast approaching.

I had accomplished what I needed to relative to giving up pot, smoking, and tobacco vaping. I was not going to go through all of the treatment in Arizona just for nothing. I told Kathy I would give them a few more days before I returned early from dropping out of treatment, and checked into the Omni Tucson National Resort, figuring I could shake off my rehab experience and have some time to myself in a nice place before heading off to prepare for married life. This was a great idea, and the Omni was a good place to do it.

It was really special to be picked up by a soulmate at the airport upon my return. I'd never had that feeling of being reunited with someone in that way; they were some of the best hugs and kisses I had ever had in my life. Kathy was surprised I arrived home tan and refreshed. She was also excited and scared to death at the same time, wondering how I would react at the reveal of all the work she had done and changes she had made at home. It was like walking into an HGTV reveal show. I was pleased with everything. My bachelor's rendering of my parents' home definitely benefited from a woman's touch. The place looked much more finished and properly outfitted. I just wondered about the cost, which would become a recurring theme between the two of us.

The work I did at rehab stuck. I wasn't really missing pot or tobacco as the weeks and months pressed on. However, as an inevitable consequence, after several weeks of my sobriety, all three of my home team core support group, Kathryn, Barbara, and Geoff, encouraged me find some pot and light up. My personality without an occasional buzz did not suit them. Nor did it really suit me for that matter. I had taken on a calm but apparently dull persona, a good look on another guy, maybe, but I guess not for me. That first toke was a relief, no doubt about it. I continued therapy locally with a new therapist and was convinced I could continue to make improvement in my moods and focus, including weed as part of the protocol.

I followed up on the recommendation of a friend, for a really good psychopharmacologist in Charleston with the hopes of finding the elusive proper cocktail of medication. My friend's son had benefited from Ketamine treatments through this guy, and perhaps I could too. The doctor explained I was not sick enough for the hallucinogenic benefit of Ketamine, but could definitely be helped by a mood stabilizer, anti- depressant, an amphetamine for daytime drowsiness and focus, and again Xanax as needed to combat any mania and sleeplessness. Years later, we still work together to manage an evolving cocktail of medicines that work properly for me.

With Kathy in my life, living in a busy household and in a relationship was a whole new set of circumstances. I realized the level of wellness I had achieved without medicines to accommodate living with bipolar disorder as a somewhat hermetic bachelor and doggie dad was not where I needed to be to maintain a healthy relationship with my future wife. As a bipolar guy, to be a good healthy husband and partner, a proper regimen of medication was key.

As the progression of my disease evolves, I definitely can still experience, even enjoy some properly moderated manic happiness, but the long bouts of depression have disappeared. It has become second nature to consciously evaluate my moods. My state of mood and mind at any given moment is for the most part demonstrated in predictable ways. Sometimes I am expressing something I think is thoughtful, which unfortunately occasionally translates to others as inappropriate.

Other times I'll fixate on something negative without good reason and find the object of my angst over it hard to shake. Other times I experience flash anger which in my case is no doubt the combination of depression and anxiety. I can turn from humming a tune, to an angry stream of loud profanities almost like a turret in a heartbeat. My mood swings are sudden, sometimes dramatic. I cycle quickly back and forth up and down throughout the day, day in and day out, all day. The barometer of my emotional backdrop can be swayed by things as simple as a TV commercial, a tune or lyric, an eyebrow raised in my direction in a negative way, or with any minutiae of the daily routines of domestic life that don't go my way. The quick mood swings are not all bad. More often than not, a commercial, tune, or other input will make me happy. The sensitive boy as I was described as a child still experiences sympathy, and empathy for others. In most of these situations, my twinge of sadness is quickly followed by a smile or the feeling of a warmed heart. Although rather than having a big heart, the trait which was projected upon me as a child, I now understand that my brain often clinically overreacts to even the smallest stimulus. The trick is being able to call yourself out on it when it happens and be open to those who love you to point it out for you when you've overlooked what I call my little bipolar blips. Even under the best-case scenario of bipolar mental health, I'm not immune from the need for a reset from time to time.

Itineraries over the next few months included yet another trip to Dayton for an engagement party given by three of Betsy's best friends. Next was another quick trip to Washington DC, for a night together in Alexandria to attend General Sullivan's Marshall Legacy Institute event. Kathy looked gorgeous in her jewels and a long tuxedo gown. I was so proud of her. I had been attending things like this alone my whole life, so to go with her on my arm took it to a new level of fun. A family wedding on Kathy's side for a nephew followed in swanky

Birmingham, Michigan, which was good timing as Hilton Head had been evacuated for another hurricane that weekend.

Next, it would be our turn. We completed all of the obligatory pre-marital counseling in the Anglican tradition. I made sure with my therapist and psychiatrist and they were both on board. There were no objections other than from a couple of disapproving friends. We visited the nearby Palmetto Bluff Resort off island in Bluffton as a potential wedding venue. Of course, she fell in love with this stunning place the minute we drove through the gates. When she heard that celebrities Justin Bieber and Haley Baldwin had booked their wedding at the same venue and would hold their big day there just weeks before our wedding date, she was hooked. The connection to one of Hollywood biggest weddings of the year was a comical sidebar for us.

Kathy did a wonderful job planning the wedding, even as her business travel took her to London, Paris, Chicago, Atlanta, Charlotte, New York and beyond. In the middle of it, she threw a long planned fiftieth all girls' birthday cruise for her sister and friends, and a 21st birthday party for her twin sons at Kiawah Island, where all of my in-laws gathered annually for Kiawah's Jazz Fest. Ironically, that year it was headlined by Gladys Knight, whom I had caught on stage years earlier with Betsy when she headlined a Dayton Philharmonic Pops concert that George had refused to attend so it was luckily forced onto me.

We decided on a small party of 45 guests, marrying at sunset in the cozy little white clapboard wedding chapel at Palmetto Bluff, the backdrop of a view of the May River. My wife looked like a goddess in her wedding dress, both the glamorous one she wore for the ceremony and the second sexier number she changed into for our reception. We hired a trio of strings and a pianist from Charleston who performed a classical repertoire mixed in with some contemporary love songs as everyone assembled in the candlelit chapel. We kept the ceremony nice and short. The musicians followed us to a cocktail hour in the River

Room at the original Palmetto Bluff Hotel, and downstairs to the wine cellar for the reveal of Kathy's wardrobe switch and our first dance to "Some Enchanted Evening." I enjoyed our classical music group, but by the time we danced the drone of the cello and violins made it sound like we were going down with the ship on the Titanic with "Nearer my God to Thee" playing.

We chose a Thursday night to avoid conflicting with everyone's Christmas plans. I have to admit, a wedding with Palmetto Bluff decorated for Christmas complete with complimentary strolling Dickens madrigal carolers is a fairytale setting. Our whole wedding weekend with family and friends could not have been more magical for them or for us. Everyone, including George, was turned out in their best black-tie finery. God Bless our dear Barbara who dressed and delivered George in a tux in his wheelchair. He gave an unexpected, terrific toast, and enjoyed the night with his sister. This was the last time he would ever be healthy enough go out with us in public, and we were all grateful for it.

After celebrating Christmas with our new blended family, we gladly headed off on our own for a honeymoon. We spent two days in London and had afternoon tea at the Savoy. My well-traveled Grandfather had called it the best hotel in the world. We went to church at Westminster Abbey in the famous pews up front, right behind St Mary's Choir. Sitting across from us, one couple was receiving bows and curtsies. Royalty in our midst was an unexpected thrill even if we couldn't figure out who they were. We hired a guide for a walking tour of Kensington Palace, Buckingham Palace, and the Mall. Kathy bought a flouncy hat at some shop that was by Royal appointment of the Queen.

From there, we traveled by car to Buckinghamshire outside London to spend the New Year at historic Cliveden House and enjoyed an English Country Manor House escape. We were sick as dogs in London, but by the time we reached the countryside, I was feeling better. Kathy took the rest of my antibiotics and fortunately we both improved enough to enjoy our surroundings and a romantic rest together. Owned by Britain's National Trust, Cliveden House and grounds are nothing short of palatial. It had once been the home of two Dukes, a Prince of Wales, and most recently, the home of the Astor family. Queen Victoria used to sail the short distance from Windsor Castle on the Thames and have tea with her neighbors at Cliveden. Kathy and I took in Windsor Castle ourselves. To stand in that Crimson Drawing Room and look out the window at the river below for anyone who appreciates history is thought provoking.

New Year's Eve at Cliveden was over the top. Kathy looked like a movie star in her gown. Another black-tie affair for us, but this time just the two of us were with a cadre of new aristocratic British acquaintances we met during our stay, a few of the ladies in tiaras. When a bagpiper came into the great hall at the stroke of midnight and played Auld Lang Syne while we danced and celebrated, everyone in the room burst into happy tears. We will never forget it. That New Year's Eve will forever be hard to top.

Just as I had given up on the prospect of marriage because of the debilitating effects of a beautiful bipolar mind, I had also long stopped envisioning myself living in something akin to the stately homes on Oakwood's west side that had so impressed me as a kid. But I'll be damned if I haven't ended up living in my dream home after all which we bought and moved into shortly after the wedding. It was just a few miles from George and Betsy's home, which once married it was obvious I should give up. Even better, I was lucky to fill it with an awesome wife, lover, companion, man's best friend in my dog, and two grown independent stepsons who as my luck would have it with my lifetime experience of privacy lived in Charleston and Ohio.

The task of combining Kathy's condo furnishings and mine was a challenge. I had to leave George and Betsy's house staged while the house was on the market until the movers rang the doorbell, packed it up and took most of it out. Kathy was an ace in accomplishment mode and overall, the move went very smoothly. Always in control, still traveling most weeks on business, and freakishly organized, Kathy had all the important items in the new house out of boxes, beds made, and furniture in place in one weekend. She could be a whiz like Betsy in this way.

Our first several weeks in the house were a struggle. Moving is a top ten stressor for just about anyone. I knew in advance, even warned Kathryn that this was going to be a trigger for the combination of depression and anxiety that would result in anger. I was right. She quickly learned what it was like to live with a bipolar person in the house, even if I was in my self-proclaimed remission from it. I tuned up my prescriptions with the pharmacologist in Charleston, who added the upper Vyvanse which we had previously considered to help with my binge eating, but at first, I had not taken it, not feeling a benefit. But when my stepsons heard I had given up on Vyvanse, they were incredulous. College kids in need of help studying were familiar with this drug which I came to realize is somewhat of a designer Ritalin. With this as encouragement I thought I would give it another try with a slightly bumped up dose.

I knew I was experiencing therapeutic effects within a few days. I had been an open mouth breather my entire life, often caught by family and friends in a moment of solitude with my mouth hanging wide open. But after a few days on Vyvanse I was clearly breathing deeply through my nose. The nose breathing helped settle and calm me. The best review I can give of my experience with Vyvanse is that I know for certain I would not have been able to sit over these last several months consistently at my laptop to write this memoir.

The combination of Vraylar and Vyvanse I was taking turned out to be a blessing for my wife. I definitely enjoyed the feeling of the Vyvanse and might double up when I needed a pick-me-up, but she could also tell when I would forget the mood stabilizer. Taking the Vyvanse I can present with "tardive dyskinesia," smacking my lips and chomping aggressively. Kathryn got a crash course in living with a mood afflicted spouse. How lucky I was to have a mate in the house who loved me and could keep me on the straight and narrow. It was for her sake that I needed to be my best after all. I would need to buck up to put my parents' house on the market, as this was going to be the next major emotional trigger. We both knew it was going to be a big one.

Then the world stopped. COVID-19. We all know what it has been like since. I had barely gotten accustomed to sharing space with Kathy. The fact that her career took her out of town two and sometimes three weeks or more a month made this a whole lot easier. When COVID hit, however, she was stuck with me 24/7. Add to that, our house would begin to fill with the twins, their girlfriends, nephews, and other friends evicted from their college dormitories. They moved in with us for short periods or even weeks at a time. Don't get me wrong, I loved every minute of this; it was what I signed up for. But the emotion of being over-peopled could be challenging. At the recommendation of my therapist, Dr. Debi, and my psychiatrist in Charleston, we added Xanax back into my medicine cabinet on an as needed basis. The world was falling apart with riots and monuments crumbling down around us. I could use the occasional dose of a happy pill to take me away.

COVID-19 has been strange here in the Carolina Lowcountry. Despite initial bad local numbers and spikes in infections, our tourist season became year-round as people flocked to the Island from densely populated cities. Like other beach and resort communities, we became a hot spot. Here, you can be outdoors year-round. You can play golf and tennis, run on the beach, ride bicycles. So, since June of 2020, things went on pretty much as usual around here, with masks up. The sad exception was that visits to George would come to an end, as his care center was closed to any and all visitors. This was awful for both of us. It was very difficult for my demented Dad to understand a pandemic, much less why he was isolated to just his one-room suite, his meals delivered to his room, no wheeling around and chatting with friends and neighbors in the corridors, no company in the dining hall, and definitely no visitors.

Kathy and I pleasantly surprised ourselves together in isolation. We kidded at the outset that we would probably end up driving each other up a wall stuck in the house alone together without a break. But we've done just great, and I think like most families cooped up together, the constant unexpected proximity literally brought us both physically and emotionally closer together.

A surprise result of the pandemic on Hilton Head was that we ended up with a hot real estate market. Within weeks after the country shut down, I had my folks' house re-staged and put it on the market at what most thought was an aggressive number. Closing on this cross generational family chapter wasn't easy on a lot of levels, but we were excited to find out what would come of it. The house went under contract quickly. The end of more than one era in our lives With this affecting my mood, I received another bombshell of a phone call, this time from Hilton Head Regional Medical Center.

George had fallen at Broad Creek, had broken his neck, and would be transferred to Memorial Hospital in Savannah during a pandemic. Damn. Poor George. Once again, however, he would rise to the occasion. After four days of driving back and forth to see him at the hospital in Savannah, he was released to rehabilitate at Broad Creek. Sadly, visits to his hospital room had been about the only time I had had the opportunity to see him in months. Twice earlier, I had sat with him at dermatology appointments to remove a skin cancer lesion on his hand, but other than that, it had been a long while since George and I had gotten any facetime. Still, he plodded along cheerfully the best he could.

My three weeks of the blues after the sale and final moving out of the family home that followed were not a surprise. We couldn't believe the volume of family possessions still left in the staged house. New owners had bought all of the furniture left behind, but another final mountain of family archives and "just can't get rid of" items filled my new man cave to the rafters. This space had become my personal refuge in my busy, full-of-family new household. It would take years to get through it all one last time. As a final adjustment to my medical regime, I contacted my psychiatrist and requested an antidepressant. He prescribed desvenlafaxine, commonly known as Pristiq. This helped me beat my blues within a week, and I have stuck with it.

As evidenced by these last waning pages, I've pretty much finally written myself up to the present day. I wonder now how to sum it all up for you. I'm seated at my little corner office in the living room of our new home, typing away. We are ready for Christmas. Our house is in tip top shape, the best we can make it. Kathy, Barbara and I worked for weeks polishing Betsy and Connie's sterling silver collection which was black when we got it out of bins. Our dining room is gleaming, displayed with Connie's China. Although the final effect is creepy and old looking, it looks like a room which needs servants to run it. My Grandparents' fine art hangs on our walls. There are old sepia photos of my great grandpa Allen with trophy fish on the walls, along with George's paintings in our guest rooms. Kathy has been busy baking, breaking out her old family recipes along with Connie Allen's date nut bread. She's baked loaves of it in bulk to give to friends and neighbors. It smells like my childhood home here at the holidays and I know my beautiful wife is doing it all to make me happy. I can assure you, it does.

About two months ago I called in Hospice to evaluate George to see if he would qualify for their palliative care programs, and Dad was given an expiration date of 6-8 weeks. Since he was considered at life's end, I could visit him at Broad Creek, and we have had happy reunions.

His sister Barbara, herself age 81, drove down from Northern Virginia to say goodbye to her big brother. We put one of those old crucifixes on his wall that slides open to reveal the candles, anointing oil, holy water, and a pack of matches with a set of instructions for the last rites. George gave himself the sign of the cross when we revealed it to him.

The last time I stopped to visit I arrived with a little Christmas tree and a couple of wrapped gifts for him to brighten up his room. I was turned away as there had been new positive COVID test results. My visits have been suspended since. Fortunately, his kind care team put the tree and presents up where he can see them from his bed. This is sad, as George can't really understand why I stopped coming again. Our only chance to visit now are Facetime calls, which he does pretty well. I'm sure now he will make it to see the New Year, 2021. Who knows? At this rate, he could live into his 90's and it wouldn't shock any of us. I just hate to see him healing time and again only to be given another knockout punch through which he will likely persevere. What a champion my Dad is.

CHAPTER 16

FULL CIRCLE

As with many bipolar projects I have started, this memoir has lingered. This is fortunate for readers as in the process of setting aside then revisiting this effort over the past nearly three years, I have put close to one hundred thousand words on the cutting room floor. As with many instincts, I'm happy with the perspective that a refreshed look at this effort has resulted in, which if nothing else is fewer words. So, I am going to pull a fast forward to conclude.

In October of 2022, I finally got the much-anticipated call. The one I had made sure my cell phone had never lost charge when inevitably the time would come. Although he had not gotten out of bed himself for 3 years since our wedding day, and the hospital bed in which he slept was only 6 inches off the floor, George fell out of bed. Hilton Head Hospital called and explained he would be transferred to Savannah Memorial again with a broken neck. Stand by, I told them. Let me get there first. I was certain we did not want a repeat of his COVID treatment and transfer there now deep into dementia at age 88. By the time I arrived at the hospital further imaging revealed that not only had he broken his neck, but also his arm, femur, and hip. He was admitted to critical care at Hilton Head where in this condition amazing George was still flirting with nurses and being his usual cheerful self although literally broken into pieces like humpty dumpty.

Unable to intubate with a widow maker of a broken neck to perform any healing surgeries on his limbs, it was time to help dad help himself to say goodbye. The decision was made to send him back to his room at Broadcreek to pass with the people there who had loved and cared for him for several years. George could die in the closet thing he had to a home, in his familiar skilled care unit. The rub with this solution was that at the nursing home they could only give him morphine orally under the tongue, and these doses were neither strong enough to ease his pain or help him towards eternal rest. My father was such an athletic stud that I believe God had given him an absolute calamity of an accident breaking four major bones in one gentle fall, yet it shouldn't have been a surprise my strong willed father survived it.

The call I prompted with the medical director at the hospice program was a jaw-dropper. "This is the correct clinical use of fentanyl." he suggested. I hesitated and was shocked. Essentially already having pulled the plug on my father's life, selecting not to risk operating, this was like pulling the plug and pushing the button and with controversial opioids for which our hometown of Dayton had become ground zero in the country's drug crisis. This was a tough position for a loving Catholic son and bipolar guy. Luckily, Kathy was on the speaker phone with the hospice doctor when the fentanyl protocol came up, and she helped me quickly go ahead with that decision. This was the right choice for all of us. My hero passed away a few days later peacefully in his room.

I went into accomplishment mode as I had for my mother's death. I had been preparing for this moment for a while. By the time he finally fell, all but the date on his headstone and funeral program had been anticipated even down to the flowers for his service which had been chosen and paid for long in advance. I took a final deep dive back into Catholic Liturgy and music and put on a proper memorial and mainly private family service at Hilton Head as a goodbye for George. All of this way more discreet than my mother's elaborate services. George and I had even joked that after all of the expense of Betsy's passing that his farewell would be beer and peanuts. The result of this planning was the largest gathering of relatives on George's side of our small family. It was a great tribute that they all showed up. Thirty-Five of us from all over the east coast gathered at our home, more than any of us had ever gathered together in one place in decades. We had a fun one-night family reunion that Kathy carefully helped me put on at home. A proper old school family wake. Sick about the reason, but happy to be together.

It was another year and a half before all of George's business affairs, and subsequently, that generation of our family was turned over with me at the wheel. Fast forward yet another 18 months, and you find me at my desk in my office in a new home. I am no longer relegated to the basement man cave like I was in the first home Kathy and I shared. We had not expected to move from the private luxury community we had settled into just after our wedding. It was exactly what we had hoped for at the time, but after a while, we found ourselves unimpressed by the trappings of our new home and small gated neighborhood with private golf, tennis, even a lock protected inland harbor and Country Club with all of the expected amenities. We made the surprising decision to downsize although to a pretty grand waterfront condominium. My view as I type looks over masts at our harbor across deep wide water looking right towards the open ocean and left towards the Atlantic Intracoastal waterway. At night mixed in with the green and red flashing maritime lights signaling the entry to our neighborhood dock, we can see the glow of the lights of Pat Conroy's sleepy Beaufort, SC. Once again, a great landing place for a bipolar guy like me.

My bipolar journey continues as it always will. My latest struggle continues to be my weight, as I am about 100 pounds overweight again, but still a lot less than in my ogre-ish years. I think one thing I'll do when I'm done here is step on a scale which I have avoided during these last couple years of post pandemic comfort eating, and get on a video chat with my therapist.

You'll barely recall that this all started as a draft for a TEDx presentation, maximum 12 minutes in length. I went over. My intent was to share my story for loved ones, caregivers, and fellow bipolar beauties who might benefit from my experience. When friends ask about what I am writing, I explain, "It's a memoir of growing up and going crazy in the upper-middle class and coming out of the dark OK on the other side." My alternate working title could be "Golden Linings Playbook." How I was able to tame the emotionally brutal beast that comes with the beautiful bipolar mind. The fact that many people I love have been unable to do so and continue to struggle gives me pause for thought, and perhaps I'll figure that out as I reread all of this as I edit. Overall, I'm just fine. Any time I think my life is or has been really tough and complicated, there is always a reminder in a nearby friend or acquaintance that millions of people have had a far rougher go than I have had. I love my life, the whole long thing, the good, the bad and the ugly of it. I can't say I wouldn't change a thing, but what's the use in that anyway? I still look at life through a bipolar lens, mainly through rose-colored lenses in hopeful happiness.

Finally, the computer screen illuminates my final thoughts as I come to a close here. I wonder for the umpteenth time if any of this will ever reach a reader or see the light of day. Folks often say, if something helps one person, the effort is worth it. Then, for that matter, my work has already served its purpose, if only selfishly. I have aired nearly all of my emotional baggage in this process, and as time passes, I expect this will continue to provide cathartic benefits. Now, my COVID memoir, which has taken me from the earliest days of the shutdown to a few years later as we ramp up to a 2024 Harris-Trump election to finish, is almost complete. Maybe, if there is any interest, I'll narrate and record the audio book in the near future. This might make for better listening than reading. I am looking forward to finding out. I'm sure with my wife supporting me, something exciting and wonderful is bound to happen. I know my knack for landing on my feet will knock something else off my bucket list, and it will be cool to find out what that is. It likely will happen in a way I haven't expected or at a time and place I could not have anticipated, like my marriage. So, I will definitely keep an eye out for it as well as continue to manifest my dreams when my bipolar mind drifts such as it can.

As I sit at my desk perched over my laptop, my fingers tingling in anticipation of typing THE END, I feel life is really just beginning for me at age 60. The way I felt at age 18, as if life is my oyster again, the world at my fingertips. Where it always was in the first place. Like at Sugar Mountain imagined by Crosby Still Nash and Young, where after twenty, life is different for a dreamer where the rubber meets the road. And yet I still have that eagerness for the future. Once again, I believe others with a brain like mine can feel this way. For all of you, I want to reaffirm. There is beauty in the bipolar brain that allows us to experience brilliance in the human condition that others with "normal" brains miss out on. Properly harnessed bipolarity can lead to wonderful experiences. I hang on to this hope for all.

With Love, I am, happily, Bipolar Bob.

****FINIT****

LIVING SUCCESSFULLY WITH BIPOLAR DISORDER

What is good mental health for someone who lives with an uncurable mental illness? What does it feel like on the other side enjoying life with a good outlook for the long haul? I have been fortunate to experience this, but do not want to let anyone off the hook. Bipolar disorder never goes away. I would be a fool to be shocked that at some point a bad mood could overwhelm me, or that a manic high could set me up for a crash with some serious consequences. Therefore, I am vigilant in a relaxed manner when it comes to my mental health. Good health of any kind rarely happens by accident.

As a fast cycler, I experience quick on the spot mood changes, all day throughout the day, every day. For the most part I have been able to put on blinders to these blips that could be graphed like the ups and downs of the stock market. I don't notice it as much anymore. Even when the tracking of my quickly changing moods might look like seismic events are happening, it feels like smooth sailing to me. I have ups and downs, highs and lows, the same as all other individuals whether they are bipolar or not. I have my upsets, including rare but bold outbursts of flash anger. The obvious result of the combination of depression and anxiety. I've been known to take my pent-up anger and angst on an unsuspecting customer service representative. Bipolarity evolves, as if trying to creep its way back in like a cancer lying in wait for a weakness. In a place of good mental health, I am fully aware of these occurrences, the reasons for them, and how to contextualize them and manage them with an eye on continuous self-improvement. Sometimes this happens easily subconsciously, other times it comes with careful consideration. My reaction time might be delayed occasionally, but I'm rarely blindsided or on the back foot when it comes to mood.

My brain works in essentially the same way as it always has since my onset pushing forty-five years ago. My bipolarity, although evolutional, has not changed. It is my response to it that has. My choice upon diagnosis was to tweak my mind with fortitude, attitude, education, medication, nutrition, exercise, and therapy, perhaps in that order of priority in my case, with medication making its way up in that line up as I age. I believe effort and desire are just as important as the drugs. To beat bipolar disorder, one must own it. Throughout my journey, I am confident I have made my own luck in figuring out how to turn bipolarity into a lifetime bonus rather than a lifetime dealbreaker.

There is innate beauty in the bipolar sensibility. Even when maudlin the bipolar brain allures us in unique and spiritual ways out of reach for many. As Picasso evolved from depression his work blossomed into bright colors, as have other famous artists had blue periods that reflected their somber moods. Mania is like a kaleidoscope of colors. I share this key message from my story one last time. I'm confident bipolar brains present us with an understanding of beauty in the human condition that others with "normal" brains miss out on. Whether it be in science, nature, faith, philosophy, business, art, or sport, and the ties that bind these in our lives, perhaps there is something we understand that others miss that indeed is sad. As I have shared before, I have come to the conclusion that I have led a creative and interesting life because of my bipolar disorder, not in spite of it.

The best nonclinical easy to understand demonstration of good mental health that speaks most to me, is an old one but a good one. Envision a treble clef and a blank piece of sheet music. Consider a normal brain plays at middle C on the musical scale. The proper place for an individual that experiences mood disorder is to strive for a level one full note above norm, just a fraction of a better mood than others experience. Even easier, if normal happiness were scored as five out of ten, then strive to be a six. The plane they used to refer to as looking at the world through rose colored glasses. Playing this tune has set me up for success and has helped me rid myself of or reduce self-destructive emotions and behaviors. This has in turn empowered me to focus on self-actualizing traits, endeavors, and relationships.

Emotions that are eliminated or reduced with a healthy bipolar perspective

- Extended periods of sullenness are gone
- No feelings of suicide or self-harm
- Reduced daytime fatigue
- No more completely self-centered thinking
- No regrets
- No feelings of envy
- Freedom from guilt
- No feeling powerless
- No need for strict privacy
- No more long periods of self-isolation
- Reduced compulsion to spend
- Fewer unfinished projects
- Reduced anxiety over bureaucracy and red tape
- Lacking pressured speech
- Reduced nighttime sleeplessness
- Reduced sleeping at inappropriate times
- Reduced interest in alcohol
- Reduced projection of personal problems onto others

- Lack of inherent pessimism
- Lack of feelings of low self-worth and low self esteem
- Lack of sense of hopelessness
- Reduced anxiety
- Reduced irritability
- Indecisiveness
- Lacking intolerance of others
- Lack of racing thoughts
- Reduced reaction to mood swings
- Lack of compulsion for risky behavior
- Lack of inappropriate conversation
- Reduced agitation
- Reduced overall body malaise
- Reduced outbursts of temper
- Reduced binge eating
- Reduced brain fog
- Reduced hoarding

Feelings and emotions that are enhanced, improved, or new with a healthy bipolar perspective:

- Positive mood
- Overall feeling of well-being
- Emotional stability
- Creativity
- Self-Awareness
- Increased empathy
- Clarity of thought
- Clarity of speech

- Improved wit
- Enjoyment of humor
- Sharper memory
- Increased attention span
- Healthy sleep
- Increased confidence
- Increased libido
- Ability to experience intimacy
- Better relationships with family
- Interest in making new friends
- Interested in joining groups
- Improved citizenship
- Improved coping skills
- Increased productivity
- Increased interest in mundane tasks
- Improved self-care
- Better grooming
- Dressing for success
- Punctuality
- Flexibility
- Vulnerability
- Motivation
- Resilience
- At peace with the past
- Ability to experience wonder in all others
- Interest in forgotten hobbies
- Willingness to try new things

- Calm
- Increased spirituality
- Increased kindness to others
- Improvement in overall cleanliness and tidiness of living conditions
- Increased wonder in nature and environment
- Rekindled ambition

I am pleased my second list of new and/or improved emotions slightly outpaces the emotions I have managed to temper or put in the past. The reduction of the negative mental integers on the first list has empowered me to focus on the positive emotions on the second list. My life perspective has transitioned from dull somber moods and some mania to a reasonably stable good mood. I no longer feel like life is a boring drag. I feel like I've come out of the dark and on the other side and experience a vivid, interesting, exciting, and thoughtful life with plenty to look forward to and share with others.

ABOUT THE AUTHOR

Bob Stavnitski experienced a seemingly idyllic childhood and enjoyed a successful, frequently stand-out high school experience as a champion athlete and all-around charismatic guy, anticipating a career in government or diplomacy. Following in his father's footsteps and those of many of his predecessors, he was becoming an "Everybody's All American" type, a most likely to succeed kind of young man. Then suddenly, his string of successes ended abruptly, and for a very long time.

Unbeknownst to Bob and his saddened and perplexed very devoted parents, his bipolar onset between the ages of 18-20, was what the medical community referred to in the 1980s as textbook timing. He would experience major unchecked deepening bipolar depression for fifteen years. By this time, he had become a two-time college dropout and had been fired from a few good positions, achieving way short of the mark that had been anticipated by his family, community, and especially himself. The fact that Bob wasn't going to make it big after all came as a surprise, but as the years passed falling short had become the long-time disappointing personal and family status quo. Mental illness never occurred to any of them.

In the hospital, after his first psychotic manic episode fueled by his first prescription for depression, the words of a psychiatrist still hung freshly in the air, "Bob, you are bipolar." It was as if a light switch had gone off and a lightbulb illuminated his brain, and suddenly it all made sense to him. Upon his diagnosis, he expressed his immediate reaction. "I'm not going to allow mental illness to take the rest of my life away from me." If only it had been that easy. Decades later, however, Bob's psychiatrists, therapists, and care team through the years share that Bob's self-awareness of his moods and mental health is acute and that Bob has been in a long recovery from bipolar disorder, in as much as it is possible for anyone that lives with a mood disorder.

Bob spares little, candidly sharing the story of his descent into madness, and eventual personal reinvention to provide hope for others living with bipolar disorder and for their loved ones, friends, and caregivers. He is convinced there is beauty, even brilliance, in the bipolar brain and soul that can enhance our understanding of the world around us and allows bipolar individuals to experience truth and beauty in the human condition including in relationships, art, nature, sport, business, in any endeavor, even faith that others with "normal" brains miss out on. Conceding sadly that redemption won't happen for everyone, Bob believes that it is possible to accomplish a sustainable comeback and make left-behind dreams become new realities.

www.ingramcontent.com/pod-product-compliance
Lightning Source LLC
Chambersburg PA
CBHW071743120626
46550CB00002B/649